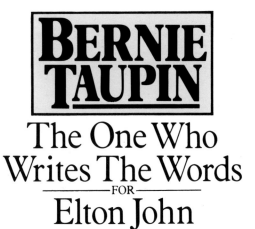

BERNIE TAUPIN

The One Who Writes The Words
—— FOR ——
Elton John

Complete Lyrics from
1968 Through to
Goodbye, Yellow Brick Road
With an Introduction
by Elton John
Illustrations by various Hands
Edited by Alan Aldridge
and Mike Dempsey

ALFRED A. KNOPF

NEW YORK

1976

With love to
Robert, Daphne, Maxine
and Elton for entirely
different reasons

Erratum

Page 108: For GOODBYE, NORMA JEAN
read CANDLE IN THE WIND

Cover illustration by
Alan Aldridge
Book designed by
Mike Dempsey
Printed and bound in Great Britain by
Westerham Press

CONTENTS

Sideways

Having been told that my doodles would
not be needed – I felt shunned!
Desperation set in. How could Taupin
put a book together without any mention
of my name! It took a few threatening
phone calls and a few broken limbs before
it was agreed to call the book 'Lyrics I
Have Written to Elton John'. Eventually
though, I was worn down by Taupin's
whimperings and his continuing habit
of wearing plaster casts. I decided to
let the little fellow have his own way –
as long as I would be permitted to
write the foreword.

Foreword

Las Vegas. (To be read in a showbiz Las
Vegas accent with plenty of drama.) The
scene is set. The launching of Bernie
Taupin's book. In line with his unique
taste in chic, he has hired Caesar's Palace
and brought in all his friends from Los
Angeles by air-conditioned rickshaw. The
room is a-buzz with anticipatory
conversations.

Lights dim – curtains rise to the music of
'The Greatest Discovery' played in big-
band style – applause. Enter Elton John
stage left – dressed in a suit made out of

Bernie Taupin book covers. The band quietly begins to play 'Your Song'. 'Ladies and gentlemen, my dear friends, Bernie – ah Bernie, you know I can remember when he used to take me into a Wimpy Bar on Oxford Street after the "Empty Sky" sessions.' Gasps from audience – uneasy fidgeting. 'But that's how Taupin is – trashy, cheap, small-time. I always managed to keep him under wraps – well out of the way – but now the little twerp wants fame, fortune, recognition of his own.'

During the last part of this spell-binding tribute, John (38, from Pinner) is seen to be tearing his hair transplant out and gradually frothing at the mouth. The audience starts to rush the exits. Sobbing frantically now, John screams at them, and as the last remaining chords of 'Your Song' echo round the now virtually empty room, the last words trickle from this pasty little troll of a man.

'And do you know – the midget can't even spell.' He hurls a copy of Taupin's book at the band and exits shouting, 'Remember "Funeral For a Friend" – huh?'

PREFACE

Hey you,
You sad-eyed old friend of mine,
There's a song that I've heard
But it's drifting away
On a wavelength that crackled and died,
And I remember the singer –
In fact he was a legend –
I've a book full of interesting names
A scratched forty-five
And so many memories,
Somehow without music it's just not the same.

Did you know
There's ghosts in the northern dance-halls,
Amplified echoes of howling young kids,
And did you see in the news
Where some radical wrote
'I'd still like to know what your rock-and-roll
Heroes did,
They'll never take our music'
But the gamblers summoned
That winter touched by fire,
And the spanner crashed in the moving parts,
Leaving us mere sparrows
Strangled on a wire.

So sad,
My poor star-tripping children,
So sad that destiny left you alone,
That a hotel sheet became a clean white shroud,
Or a twisted wreck your final home.
It was simple to us,
We were born children of fate
Sold to the world in twelve-inch frames,
Given our tickets,
Herded to heaven in a private plane.

But unmistaken
The music soared above us.
Its power upon the masses never died,
But when our systems fed the voice
It was the words upon his lips
That made the crowds that watched him cry.

WHEN THE FIRST TEAR SHOWS

Hold my hand, girl, tighter,
Much much tighter,
'Cause what I've got to say
I only hope and pray
Comes out as well as I rehearsed it yesterday.

And baby, when the first tear shows,
It's a sign for you to go,
And baby, when the first tear shows,
It's a sign for you to go
And leave her alone
With the broken dreams that she owns.

It's a crime for me to tell you,
It's a sin for me to stay,
And I'll never look behind me
When I start to walk away;
Girl, I'm sorry,
But it's all that I can say.

You know that I used to love you so;
We enjoyed every moment together,
Well, I'm not the kind of man
To for ever hold your hand;
And I've said as much as I can say.

TURN TO ME

Turn to me, turn to me,
When you're lonely;
Brush them aside, gather your pride,
And baby, turn to me.

Don't listen to the people
Who spread lies about your name;
I know it hurts, but baby I've had it too;
I've learned to live with their abuse,
I've learned to live with those who choose
To disregard my emptiness and lose me.

Your laughter has died in the heat of the night,
And the people, they pretend that company is
        bright;
But brighter you'll wait by the phone that has died,
Don't build up your hopes,
There's no one left for you to confide in.

But you seem to be happy
Just now to go on;
I can see through them, baby,
Can't you see what is wrong?
You're hurting yourself more than you'll ever
        know,
You're pushing the people to tell you to go.

10

12

THE TIDE WILL TURN FOR REBECCA

Can you hear the floorboards crying
In a room on the second floor
That used to be owned by someone who's no one,
But he don't live there any more?

Only Rebecca clasping her head on her knees,
Trying to work out what it's about,
And why someone had to leave.

But dry up your tears,
Stop counting the years;
Don't worry what's coming,
Forget all your fears.

And the tide will turn for Rebecca –
And the tide will turn for Rebecca –
Her life will change,
Her hopes rearrange
Into something that might really matter.

TAKING THE SUN FROM MY EYES

Don't you worry where I'm going,
I'll just go without you knowing,
I won't come back to you again;
I'll leave right now,
And catch the train.

Don't you wait for me any more,
I loved you then,
And then I was sure;
Our love was something at the start,
You killed the sun
And broke my heart.

Oh why, oh why, did you do it?
I thought I'd never get through it,
While you were telling me lies,
You were taking the sun –
Taking the sun from my eyes.

So just listen to me while I say,
Forget all the love of those days;
They're only empty and they're gone,
Just like the river that's washed in the storm.

13

SEASON OF THE RAIN

IT'S ME THAT YOU NEED

Ice thaws the sun when autumn comes,
And Bristol trips and buggy rides are over,
And the nucleus of everyone has disappeared,
As winter holds my shoulder.

So put on your make-up,
Make up to me now;
Kick off your sand-shoes,
Throw them in the sea now,
It's the season of the rain.

You wear your big hat,
I'll wear my check cap,
Throw up your string bags
Into the old trap.
It's the season of the rain,
And I gotta go home –
I wanna go home again.

Castles in the country,
See the maids of air;
Rambling fires and canopies contain us,
And the waters of the countryside
Wash away our cares –
Leave the city lights behind us.

Hey there – look in the mirror,
Are you afraid you might see me looking at you?
Waiting, waiting at windows,
Oh, it's me that you need.
Yes, it's me, and I'm waiting for you.

But I'll remain silent,
Oh, I won't say a word,
I'll leave you to realize
I'm the light in your world.

And it's me, yes, it's me,
Yes, it's me, yes, it's me, that you're needing,
It's me, yes, it's me,
Yes, it's me, yes, it's me that you need.
Yes, it's me, yes, it's me,
Yes, it's me if you want to be living,
I'm the one who's forgiving,
Admit that it's me that you need.

Watching, watching the swallows fly,
It all means the same.
Just like them, you can fly home again:
But don't, don't forget yesterday;
Pride is an ugly word, girl,
And you still know my name.

14

16

ROCK-AND-ROLL MADONNA

If anyone should see me making it down the
    highway,
Breaking all the laws of the land,
Well, don't you try to stop me, I'm going her way,
And that's the way I'm sure she had it planned.

Well, that's my rock-and-roll Madonna,
She's always been a lady of the road;
Well, everybody wants her,
But no one ever gets her,
Well, the freeway is the only way she knows.

Well, if she would only slow down for a short while
I'd get to know her just before she leaves,
But she's got some fascination for that two-wheel
    combination,
And I swear it's going to be the death of me.

LADY SAMANTHA

When the shrill winds are screaming, and the
    evening is still,
Lady Samantha glides over the hill
In a long satin dress that she wears every day;
Her home is the hillside, her bed is the grave.

Lady Samantha glides like a tiger
Over the hills with no one beside her,
No one comes near,
They all live in fear,
But Lady Samantha, she sheds only tears.

The tales that are told round the fire every night
Are out of proportion, and none of them right;
She is harmless and empty of anything bad,
For she once had something that most of you have.

17

Empty sky.
M. a. Taupin

EMPTY SKY

I'm not a rat to be spat upon,
Locked up in this room.
Those bars that look towards the sun
At night look towards the moon.

Every day the swallows play
In the clouds of love –
Make me wish that I had wings,
Take me high above.

And I looked high,
Saw the empty sky,
If I could only –
Could only fly.

I'd drift with them
In endless space
But no man flies
From this place.

At night I lie upon my bench
And stare towards the stars,
The cold night air comes creeping in,
And home seems oh, so far.

If I could only swing
Upon those twinkling dots above,
I'd look down from the heavens
Upon the ones I love.

Hey, the lucky locket
Hangs around your precious neck,
Some luck I ever got with you,
And I wouldn't like to bet

That sooner or later you'll own
Just one half of this land
By shining your eyes on the wealth
Of every man.

Just send up my love,
Ain't seen nothing but tears,
Now I've got myself
In this room for years.

VALHALLA

The seadogs have all sailed their ships
Into the docks of dawn,
While the sirens sit
And comb their hair
And twiddle with their thumbs.

Oh! Thor above the mountain,
Look down upon your children;
This is their heaven,
Where they're told
To bring their galleons.

Seek, you find your place with me,
Men of iron, men of steel;
Only the brave hear the hammers ring
In the courts of the Queens,
In the halls of the Kings.

You can come to Valhalla
In your own time,
Come to Valhalla,
Seek and you will find
Valhalla.

There's long-boats in the harbour
Which arrive there every hour
With the souls of the heroes
Whose blood lies on the flowers.

And this heaven is the home
Of every man who loves his sword,
And he uses it for freedom
To preach the word of Thor.

20

HYMN 2000

She chose the soft centre
And took it to bed with her mother,
And the ideal confusion
Was just an illusion
To gain further news of her brother.

And the comfort of mother
Was just an appeal for protection,
For the cat from next door
Was found later at four
In surgical dissection.

And I don't want to be
The son of any freak
Who for a chocolate centre
Can take you off the street.

For soon they'll plough the desert,
And God knows where I'll be,
Collecting submarine numbers
On the main street of the sea.

The Vicar is thicker,
And I just can't see through to him,
For his cardinal sings
A collection of hymns,
And a collection of coins
Is made after.

And who wrote the Bible,
Was it Judas or Pilate?
Well, one cleans his hands
While the other one hangs,
But still I continue to stand.

WESTERN FORD GATEWAY

It's hard to feel what's in your hand
Where the gas-lamps grow
And the garbage blows
Around the paper stands.

And a baby cried
And I saw a light
And I wondered where
And I wondered why
There'd be a loss of life
Down here tonight.

Down on Western Ford Gateway,
That's a place where the dead say
That a man lives no more
Than his fair share of days,
Down on Western Ford Gateway.

It flowed upon the cobbled floor
For the bottle's dead,
And they're drunk again
By the tavern door.

GULLIVER

Gulliver's gone
To the final command of his master;
His watery eyes had washed
All the hills with his laughter;
And the seasons can change
All the light from the grey to the dim,
But the light in his eyes
Will see no more so bright
As the sheep
That he locked in the pen.

There's four feet of ground
In front of the barn
That's sun-baked and rain-soaked
And part of the farm;
But now it lies empty,
So cold and so bare,
Gulliver's gone
But his memory lies there.

By-passing the doors of his life
Was a stage I remember,
And in later years
He would cease to bare teeth to a stranger;
For sentiment touched him,
As cyclamen holds him,
And later men came from the town,
Who said, 'Clear the child
This won't take a while,'
And Gulliver's gone with the dawn.

23

LADY, WHAT'S TOMORROW?

Look up, little brother –
Can you see the clover?
No, not over there, a little bit left,
And over there.

Now look and see the lilac tree,
The lily pond, the skylark's song,
The open air, but no one cares
If branches live and die out there.

Remember when you were nine
And I was ten,
We would run into the woods?
No, we never will again.

And, lady, what's tomorrow,
What's tomorrow anyway?
If it's not the same as now,
It's the same as yesterday.

Yes, lady, what's tomorrow,
Will it be the same as now,
Will the farmer push the pen,
Will the writer pull the plough?

Look up, little brother –
Can you see the clover?
Oh, sorry but it's over,
Now there's concrete and no clover.

SAILS

I viewed in my presence
My hand on my forehead,
And sighting the liners
Of mad merchant seamen
In search of the living,
Or the spices of China.

Lucy walked gently
Between the damp barrels,
And shut out my eyes
With the width of her fingers,
Said she's guessed the number
Of bales in the back-room.

While the sea-gulls were screaming
Lucy was eating;
Then we hauled up our colours
The way The Mother had told us,
And together we just watched the sails.

'Lucy,' I said
In a passage of cotton kegs,
'Can we hold hands,
I'm sure that it's warmer?'
Then the gulls ate the crumbs
Of Lucy's sandwich.

24

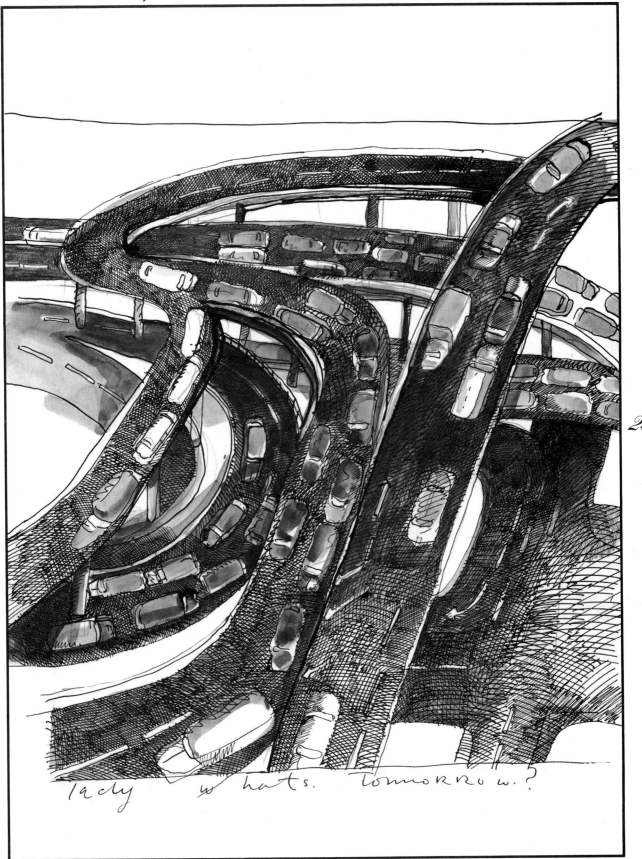

lady w hats. Tomorrow.?

SKYLINE PIGEON

Turn me loose from your hands,
Let me fly to distant lands,
Over green fields, trees and mountains,
Flowers and forest fountains,
Home along the lanes of the skyway –

For this dark and lonely room
Projects a shadow cast in gloom,
And my eyes are mirrors
Of the world outside;
Thinking of the way
That the wind can turn the tide,
And these shadows turn
From purple into grey.

For just a Skyline Pigeon,
Dreaming of the open,
Waiting for the day
He can spread his wings
And fly away again:
Fly away, Skyline Pigeon, fly
Towards the dreams
You've left so very far behind.

Just let me wake up in the morning,
To the smell of new-mown hay,
To laugh and cry, to live and die,
In the brightness of my day.

I want to hear the pealing bells
Of distant churches sing,
But most of all please free me
From this aching metal ring,
And open out this cage towards the sun.

THE SCAFFOLD

In Orient where wise I was
To please the way I live,
Come give the beggar chance at hand,
His life is on his lip.

Three score a thousand times
Where once in Amazon,
Where Eldorado holds the key,
No keeper holds my hand.

Unchain the gate of solitude,
The ruler says you run,
Run hard unto the scaffold high,
It's your chance to jump the gun.

Oh, how high the scaffold grows!
The plant life of your widow
In black-lace curtains brought you near,
From out the plate-glass window.

The Minotaur with bloody hands
Is enraged by the sun,
Caged he by the corpses,
Brought forth by the dawn.

In Orient is as I told,
The buckshee hangman swears,
For open crypts to silence,
Nylon knots to sway by prayer.

In Orient where wise I was
To please the way I live,
Come give the beggar chance at hand,
His life is on his lip.

26

27

lton John was born in Pinner
iddlesex and has Played the
iano since he was a little
oy he likes football and
s millions of Pairs of glasses

YOUR SONG

It's a little bit funny, this feeling inside,
I'm not one of those who can easily hide,
I don't have much money, but boy if I did,
I'd buy a big house where we both could live.

If I was a sculptor, but then again no,
Or a man who makes potions in a travelling show,
I know it's not much, but it's the best I can do,
My gift is my song and this one's for you.

And you can tell everybody this is your song,
It may be quite simple but now that it's done
I hope you don't mind, I hope you don't mind,
That I put down in words,
How wonderful life is while you're in the world.

I sat on the roof and kicked off the moss,
Well, a few of the verses, well, they've got me
    quite cross,
But the sun's been quite kind while I wrote this
    song,
It's for people like you, that keep it turned on.

So excuse me forgetting, but these things I do,
You see I've forgotten if they're green or they're
    blue,
Anyway, the thing is what I really mean,
Yours are the sweetest eyes I've ever seen.

30

I NEED YOU TO TURN TO

You're not a ship to carry my life,
You are naked to my love in many lonely nights.

I've strayed from the cottages and found myself
    here,
For I need your love, your love protects my fears.

And I wonder sometimes, and I know I'm unkind,
But I need you to turn to when I act so blind,
And I need you to turn to when I lose control,
You're my guardian angel who keeps out the cold.

Did you paint your smile on, well I said I knew
That my reason for living was for loving you?

We're related in feeling, but you're high above,
You're pure and you're gentle with the grace of a
    dove.

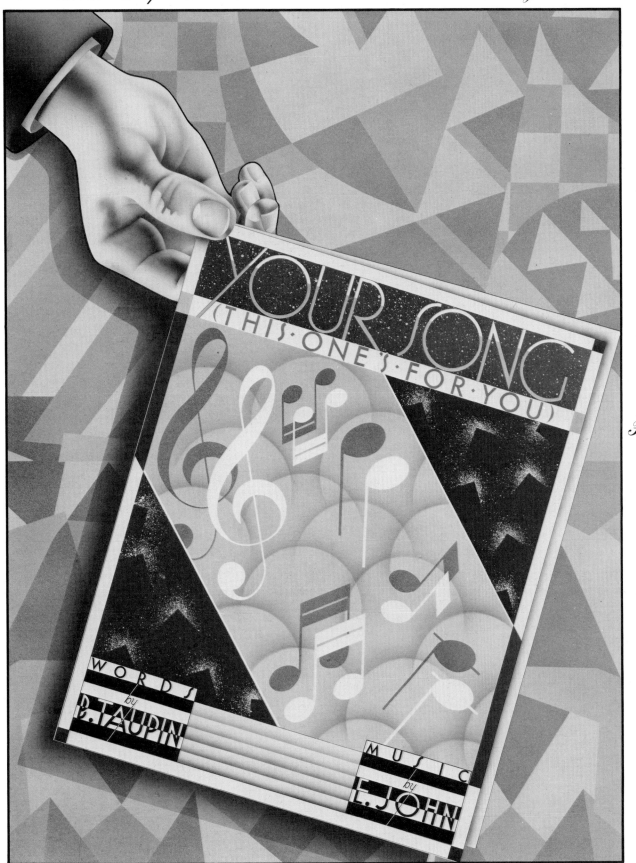

32

NO SHOESTRINGS ON LOUISE

Lady Love rides a big red Cadillac,
Buys the hoe-down show, salt and beans,
Goes to the church to pray for Lucifer,
She milked the male population clean.

So ride in the line, shake yourself by the hand,
Live your life inside a paper can,
But you'll never get to pick and choose,
She's bought you and sold you,
There ain't no shoestrings on Louise.

Come on down, come on down from the ladder,
Henry, get your head out of the clouds,
What she wants is to go kissing on a swine-herd –
You might as well kiss the boss man's cow.

All those city women want to make us poor men,
And this land's got the worse for the worrying;
I got married at the early age of fourteen,
And I've been worrying about the way you all
        been loving 'em.

THE KING MUST DIE

No man's a jester playing Shakespeare
Round your throne-room floor,
While the juggler's act is danced upon
The crown that you once wore.

And sooner or later
Everybody's kingdom must end,
And I'm so afraid your courtiers
Cannot be called best friends.

Caesar's had your troubles,
Widows had to cry,
While mercenaries in cloisters sing,
And the King must die.

Some men are better staying sailors,
Take my word and go;
But tell the ostler that his name was
The very first they chose.

And if my hands are stained for ever,
And the altar should refuse me,
Would you let me in, would you let me in,
Should I cry sanctuary?

Caesar's had your troubles,
Widows had to cry,
While mercenaries in cloisters sing,
And the King must die.

No man's a jester playing Shakespeare
Round your throne-room floor,
While the juggler's act is danced upon
The crown that you once wore.

The King is dead
The King is dead
The King is dead
Long Live the King.

33

FIRST EPISODE AT HIENTON

I was one as you were one,
And we were two so much in love for ever;
I loved the white socks that you wore,
But you don't wear white socks no more,
Now you're a woman.

I joked about your turned-up nose
And criticized your schoolgirl clothes,
But would I then have paced these roads to love
    you?

For seasons come and seasons go,
Bring forth the rain, the sun and snow,
Make Valerie a woman –
And Valerie is lonely.

No more to roam on the snow hills of Hienton,
Undecided with the guardians of the older
    generation;
A doormat was a sign of welcome
In the winter months to come;
And in the summer laughing
Through the castle ruins we'd run.

For the quadrangle sang to the sun
And the grace of our feeling,
And the candle burned low as we talked of the
    future
Underneath the ceiling.

There were tears in the sky,
And the clouds in your eyes were just cover,
For your thighs were the cushions
Of my love and yours for each other.

For seasons come and seasons go,
Bring forth the rain, the sun and snow,
Make Valerie a woman –
And Valerie is lonely.

The songs still are sung,
It was fun to be young,
But please don't be sad where'ere you are –
I am who I am,
You are who you are –
Now Valerie's a woman
Now Valerie's a woman
Now Valerie's a woman.

SIXTY YEARS ON

Who'll walk me down to church when I'm sixty
    years of age,
When the ragged dog they gave me has been ten
    years in the grave,
And senorita play guitar play it just for you
My rosary has broken and my beads have all
    slipped through.

You've hung up your greatcoat and you've laid
    down your gun,
You know the war you fought in wasn't too much
    fun.

And the future you're giving me holds nothing
    for a gun,
I've no wish to be living sixty years on.

Yes I'll sit with you and talk let your eyes relive
    again,
I know my vintage prayers would be very much
    the same,
And Magdelena plays the organ plays it just for
    you
Your choral lamp that burns so low when you are
    passing through.

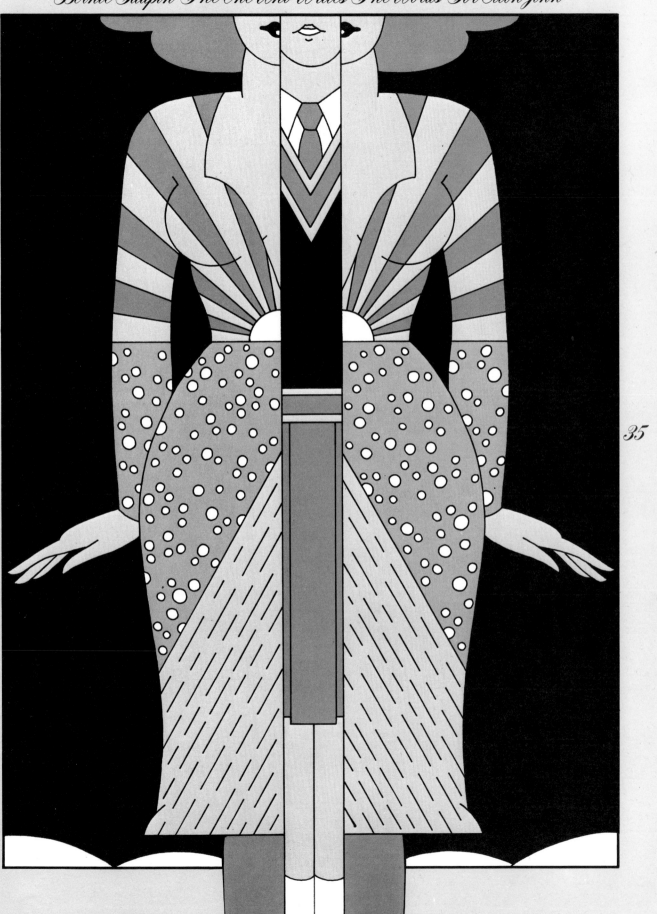

35

36

THE CAGE

Have you ever lived in a cage
Where you live to be whipped and be tamed?
For I've never loved in a cage,
Or talked to a friend or just waved.

Well, I walk while they talk about virtue,
Just raised on my back legs and snarled,
Watched you kiss your old daddy with passion,
And tell dirty jokes as he died.

But I'm damned when I really care there,
For the cellar's the room in your lives
Where you lace yourself with bad whisky,
And close the cage doors on your life.

Well, I pray while you bathe in bad water,
Sing songs that I learnt as a boy,
Then break all the bones in my body
On the bars you can never destroy.

Have you ever lived in a cage
Where you live to be whipped and be tamed?
For I've never loved in a cage,
Or talked to a friend or just waved.

TAKE ME TO THE PILOT

If you feel that it's real
I'm on trial,
And I'm here in your prison,
Like a coin in your mint,
I am dented and spent with high treason.

Through a glass eye your throne
Is the one danger zone,
Take me to the Pilot for control,
Take me to the Pilot of your soul,
Take me to the Pilot,
Lead me to his chamber,
Take me to the Pilot,
I am but a stranger.

Well, I know he's not old, and I'm told he's a
    virgin,
For he may be she,
But what I'm told is never for certain.

BORDER SONG

Holy Moses, I have been removed;
I have seen the spectre, he has been here too;
Distant cousin from down the line,
Brand of people who ain't my kind,
Holy Moses, I have been removed.

Holy Moses, I have been deceived;
Now the wind has changed direction and I'll have
    to leave;
Won't you please excuse my frankness, but it's
    not my cup of tea,
Holy Moses, I have been deceived.

I'm going back to the border,
Where my affairs, my affairs ain't abused,
I can't take any more bad water,
I've been poisoned from my head down to my
    shoes,
Holy Moses, I have been deceived.

Holy Moses, let us live in peace,
Let us strive to find a way to make all hatred
    cease:
There's a man over there, what's his colour,
    I don't care;
He's my brother, let us live in peace,
He's my brother, let us live in peace,
He's my brother, let us live in peace.

37

BALLAD OF A WELL-KNOWN GUN

I pulled out my Stage Coach Times and I read
    the latest news,
I tapped my feet in dumb surprise, and of course
    they knew;
The Pinkertons, they pulled out my bags and
    asked me for my name,
I stuttered out my answer and hung my head in
    shame.

Now they've found me, at last they've found me,
It's hard to run from a starving family,
Now they've found me I won't run,
I'm tired of hearing,
    There goes a well-known gun.

Now I've seen this chain-gang, let me see my
    priest,
I couldn't have faced your desert sand,
    old burning brown-backed beast;
The poor house they hit me for my kin,
    and claimed my crumbling walls,
Now I know how Reno felt when he ran from
    the law.

AMOREENA

Lately I've been thinking how much I miss my
    lady,
Amoreena's in the cornfield brightening the
    daybreak,
Living like a lusty flower, running through the
    grass for hours,
Rolling through the hay like a puppy child.

And when it rains the rain falls down
Washing out the cattle town;
And she's far away somewhere in her eiderdown,
And she dreams of crystal streams,
Of days gone by when we would lean
Laughing fit to burst upon each other.

I can see you sitting eating apples in the evening,
The fruit juice flowing slowly, slowly, slowly,
Down the bronze of your body,
Living like a lusty flower, running through the
    grass for hours,
Rolling through the hay like a puppy child.

And when it rains the rain falls down
Washing out the cattle town;
And she's far away somewhere in her eiderdown,
And she dreams of crystal streams,
Of days gone by when we would lean
Laughing fit to burst upon each other.

Oh, if only I could nestle in the cradle of your
    cabin,
My arms around your shoulders, the windows
    wide and open;
While the swallow and the sycamore are playing
    in the valley,
I miss you, Amoreena, like a king bee misses
    honey.

40

SON OF YOUR FATHER

You're the son of your father,
Try a little bit harder,
Do for me as he would do for you,
With blood and water, bricks and mortar,
He built you a home;
You're the son of your father,
So treat me as your own.

Well, slowly Joseph, he lowered the rifle
And he emptied out the shells,
Van Bushell he come towards him,
He shook his arm and wished him well.

He said, 'Now hey, blind man, that is fine,
But I sure can't waste my time,
So move aside and let me go my way,
I've got a train to ride.'

Well, Joseph turned around,
His grin was now a frown,
He said, 'Let me just refresh your mind,
Your manners, boy, seem hard to find.'

There's two men lying dead as nails
On an East Virginia farm,
For charity's an argument
That only leads to harm.

So be careful when they're kind to you,
Don't you end up in the dirt,
Just remember what I'm saying to you
And you likely won't get hurt.

COUNTRY COMFORT

Soon the pines will be falling everywhere,
Village children fight each other for a share;
And the six-o-nine goes roaring past the creek,
Deacon Lee prepares his sermon for next week.

I saw Grandma yesterday down at the store,
Well, she's really going fine for eighty-four,
Well, she asked me if some time I'd fix her barn,
Poor old girl, she needs a hand to run the farm.

And it's good old country comfort in my bones,
Just the sweetest sound my ears have ever known,
Just an old-fashioned feeling fully-grown,
Country comfort's any truck that's going home.

Down at the well they've got a new machine,
Foreman says it cuts man-power by fifteen,
But that ain't natural, well, so old Clay would say,
You see he's a horse-drawn man until his dying
     day.

Now the old fat goose is flying 'cross the sticks,
The hedgehog's done in clay between the bricks,
And the rocking-chair's a-creakin' on the porch,
Across the valley moves the herdsman with his
     torch.

MY FATHER'S GUN

From this day on I own my father's gun;
We dug his shallow grave beneath the sun,
I laid his broken body down below the southern
    land,
It wouldn't do to bury him where any Yankee
    stands.

I'll take my horse and I'll ride the northern plain
To wear the colour of the greys and join the fight
    again,
Oh, I'll not rest until I know the cause is fought
    and won;
From this day on until I die I'll wear my
    father's gun.

I'd like to know where the riverboat sails tonight,
To New Orleans, well, that's just fine all right
'Cos there's fighting there and the company
    needs men,
So slip us a rope and sail on round the bend.

As soon as this is over we'll go home
To plant the seeds of justice in our bones,
To watch the children growing and see the
    women sewing –
There'll be laughter when the bells of freedom
    ring.

TALKING OLD SOLDIERS

Why, hello, say, can I buy you another glass of
    beer?
Well, thanks a lot, that's kind of you,
It's nice to know you care.
These days there's so much going on,
No one seems to wanna know;
I may be just an old soldier to some,
But I know how it feels to grow old.

Yeah, that's right,
You can see me here most every night;
You'll always see me staring
At the walls and at the lights,
Funny, I remember – oh, it's years ago I'd say –
I'd stand at that bar
With my friends who've passed away
And drink three times the beer that I can drink
    today;
Yes, I know how it feels to grow old.

I know what they're saying, son,
There goes old mad Joe again;
Well, I may be mad at that, I've seen enough
To make a man go out his brains;
Well, do they know what it's like
To have a graveyard as a friend?
'Cos that's where they are, boy, all of them,
Don't seem likely I'll get friends like that again.

Well, it's time I moved off,
But it's been great just listening to you;
And I might even see yer next time I'm passing
    through –
You're right, there's so much going on,
No one seems to wanna know;
So keep well, keep well, old friend,
And have another drink on me;
Just ignore all the others, you've got your
    memories.

44

46

WHERE TO NOW, ST PETER?

I took myself a blue canoe,
And I floated like a leaf;
Dazzling, dancing,
Half-enchanted,
In my Merlin sleep.

Crazy was the feeling,
Restless were my eyes,
Insane they took the paddles,
My arms they paralysed.

So where to now, St Peter,
If it's true I'm in your hands?
I may not be a Christian
But I've done all one man can;
I understand I'm on the road
Where all that was is gone,
So where to now, St Peter?
Show me which road I'm on,
Which road I'm on.

It took a sweet young foreign gun,
This lazy life is short,
Something for nothing always ending
With a bad report.

Dirty was the daybreak,
Sudden was the change,
In such a silent place as this,
Beyond the rifle range.

BURN DOWN THE MISSION

You tell me there's an angel in your tree,
Did he say he'd come to call on me?
For things are getting desperate in our home,
Living in the parish of the restless folks I know.

Bring your family down to the riverside,
Look to the east to see where the fat stock hide;
Behind four walls of stone the rich man sleeps,
It's time we put the flame-torch to their keep.

Burn down the mission
If we're gonna stay alive,
Watch the black smoke fly to heaven,
See the red flame light the sky.

Burn down the mission,
Burn it down to stay alive,
It's our only chance of living,
Take all you need to live inside.

Deep in the woods the squirrels are out today,
My wife cried when they came to take me away,
But what more could I do just to keep her warm
Than burn, burn, burn, burn down the mission
    walls.

COME DOWN IN TIME

In the quiet silent seconds I turned off the
    light-switch,
And I came down to meet you in the half-light
    the moon left,
While a cluster of nightjars sang some songs out
    of tune,
A mantle of bright light shone down from a room.

'Come down in time,' I still hear her say,
So clear in my ear like it was today,
'Come down in time,' was the message she gave,
'Come down in time and I'll meet you half way.'

Well, I don't know if I should have heard her as
    yet,
But a true love like hers is a hard love to get,
And I've walked most all the way and I ain't
    heard her call,
And I'm getting to thinking if she's coming at all.

'Come down in time,' I still hear her say,
So clear in my ear like it was today,
'Come down in time,' was the message she gave,
'Come down in time and I'll meet you half way.'

There are women and women and some hold you
    tight,
While some leave you counting the stars in the
    night.

47

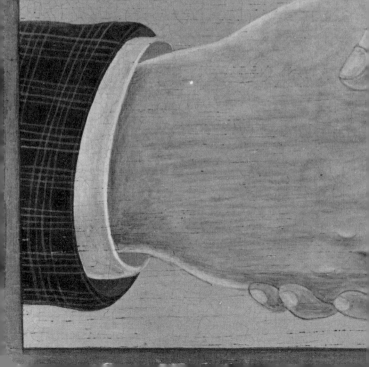
FRI

NDS

CAN I PUT YOU ON?

I work in the foundry for a penny and a half a day,
Like a blind street-musician I never see those
    who pay.
It's dirty work in Birmingham,
Better deal for a Sheffield man,
If he can rivet, then his kids can buy
Candy from the candy man.

And the van that comes round weekends
Selling fancy city things,
Sold by the man in the trilby hat
And whiskers spread like wings.
You can hear him sing,
Oh, you can hear him sing –
Can I put you on?
People, can I put you on?
Tell you that I love you, people,
Sing a salesman's song,
And put you on.

And a second cousin works the pits in Newcastle
    on Tyne,
And he don't care if it rains outside, there's
    coal-dust on his mind.
It's dirty work in Manchester,
But the crew gets paid its gelt
Bang on the bell on Friday,
You buys a little something for yourself.

FRIENDS

I hope the day will be a lighter highway,
For friends are found on every road;
Can you ever think of any better way
For the lost and weary travellers to go?

Making friends for the world to see,
Let the people know you've got what you need;
With a friend at hand you will see the light,
If your friends are there, then everything's
    all right.

It seems to me a crime that we should age,
These fragile times should never slip us by;
A time you never can or shall erase
As friends together watch their childhood fly.

52

MICHELLE'S SONG

Cast a pebble on the water,
Watch the ripples gently spreading,
Tiny daughter of the Camargue,
We were meant to be together.
We were made for one another
In a time it takes to grow up,
If only we were old enough
Then they might leave us both alone,

So take my hand in your hand,
Say it's great to be alive,
No one's going to find us
No matter how they try,
No one's going to find us,
It's wonderful so wild beneath the sky.

Sleeping in the open,
See the shadows softly moving,
Take a train towards the southlands,
Our time was never better.
We shall pass such sights of splendour
On the door of a new life,
It had to happen soon I guess,
Whether it is wrong or it is right.

We learned to be so graceful
Watching wild horses running,
And from those agile angels
We knew the tide was turning.
For we watched as on the skyway
The herons circled slowly,
While we mere mortals watched them fly
Our sleepless eyes grew heavy.

HONEY ROLL

If you want to try to ride me on your pony,
Loosen up my tie to help me breathe,
Insisting that I pay my alimony,
Each and every day's the same old scene.

Come on, do the roll, do the roll with me,
Come on, do the roll, do the roll with me;
I said honey, I said honey,
I said honey, I said honey,
Come on, do the honey roll with me.

Well, I want to say that I'm your Mister Funky,
Singing the song that's taking up your time;
I did the dog, and now I'm your funky monkey,
Sing it children, sing it of your mind.

SEASONS

For our world the circle turns again;
Throughout the year we've seen the seasons
        change;
It's meant a lot to me to start anew –
Oh, the winter's cold, but I'm so warm with you.

Out there there's not a sound to be heard;
And the seasons seem to sleep upon their words
As the waters freeze up with the summer's end –
Oh, it's funny how young lovers start as friends.

53

Peter Heard.

LEVON

Levon wears his war-wound like a crown,
He calls his child Jesus 'cause he likes the name
And he sends him to the finest school in town.

Levon, Levon likes his money,
He makes a lot they say;
Spends his days counting
In a garage by the motorway.

He was born a pauper to a pawn on a Christmas
 day,
When the New York Times
Said, 'God is dead, and war's begun,
And Alvin Tostig has a son today.'

And he shall be Levon,
And he shall be
A good man,
And he shall be
Levon,
In tradition with
The family plan,
And he shall be
Levon,
And he shall
Be a good man,
He shall be
Levon.

Levon sells cartoon balloons in town,
His family business thrives.
Jesus blows up balloons all day,
Sits on the porch swing watching them fly,
And Jesus, he wants to go to Venus,
Leave Levon far behind;
Take a balloon,
And go sailing,
While Levon –
Levon
Slowly
Dies.

TINY DANCER

Blue-jean baby,
L.A. lady, seamstress for the band,
Pretty-eyed, pirate smile, you'll marry a music
 man.
Ballerina, you must have seen her dancing in the
 sand,
And now she's in me, always with me, Tiny
 Dancer in my hand.

Jesus freaks
Out in the streets
Handing tickets out for God;
Turning back she just laughs,
The boulevard is not that bad.

Piano man
He makes his stand
In the auditorium;
Looking on
She sings the songs,
The words she knows,
The tune she hums.

But oh,
How it feels so real lying here
With no one near,
Only you, and you can hear me
When I say softly, slowly –

Hold me closer, Tiny Dancer,
Count the headlights
On the highway;
Lay me down in sheets of linen,
You had a busy day today.

56

58

RAZOR FACE

Has anybody here seen Razor Face?
Heard he's back lookin' for a place to lay down;
Must be getting on,
Needs a man who's young to walk him round,
Needs a man who's young to walk him round.

Oh, it must be hard for the likes of you
To get by in a world that you just can't see
    through,
And it looks so cold.
How does it feel to know you can't go home?
How does it feel to know you can't go home?

Come on, Razor Face, my old friend,
I'll meet you down by the truck stop inn
With a bottle of booze in the back of my car,
You're a song on the lips of an ageing star.

Razor Face, amazing grace
Protects you like a glove
And I'll never learn the reason why
I love your Razor Face.

GOODBYE

And now that it's all over
The birds can nest again.
I'll only snow when the sun comes out,
I'll shine only when it starts to rain.

And if you want a drink,
Just squeeze my hand, and wine will flow into the
    land
And feed my lambs.

For I am a mirror,
I can reflect the moon,
I will write songs for you,
I'll be your silver spoon.

I'm sorry I took your time,
I am the poem that doesn't rhyme.
Just turn back a page,
I'll waste away –
I'll waste away –
I'll waste away.

MADMAN ACROSS THE WATER

I can see very well,
There's a boat on the reef with a broken back
And I can see it very well;
There's a joke and I know it very well,
It's one of those that I told you long ago,
Take my word, I'm a madman, don't you know?

Once a fool had a good part in the play,
If it's so, would I still be here today?
It's quite peculiar in a funny sort of way,
They think it's very funny everything I say;
Get a load of him, he's so insane,
You'd better get your coat, dear,
It looks like rain.

We'll come again next Thursday afternoon,
The in-laws hope they'll see you very soon;
But is it in your conscience that you're after
Another glimpse of the Madman across the Water?

I can see very well,
There's a boat on the reef with a broken back
And I can see it very well;
There's a joke and I know it very well,
It's one of those that I told you long ago,
Take my word, I'm a madman, don't you know?

We'll come again next Thursday afternoon,
The in-laws hope they'll see you very soon;
But is it in your conscience that you're after
Another glimpse of the Madman across the Water?

The ground's a long way down but I need more,
Is the nightmare black
Or are the windows painted?
Will they come again next week –
Can my mind really take it?

59

INDIAN SUNSET

As I awoke this evening, with the smell of
  woodsmoke clinging
Like a gentle cobweb hanging upon a painted
  tepee;
Oh, I went to see my chieftain with my war-lance
  and my woman,
For he told us that the yellow moon would very
  soon be leaving.

This I can't believe, I said, I can't believe our
  Warlord's dead,
Oh, he would not leave the chosen ones to the
  buzzards and the soldiers' guns.

Oh, great father of the Iroquois, ever since I was
  young I've
Read the writings of the smoke, and breast-fed
  on the sound of drums.
I've learned to hurl the tomahawk and ride a
  painted pony
Wild, To run the gauntlet of the Sioux to make a
  chieftain's daughter mine.

And now you ask that I should watch the red
  man's race be slowly crushed;
What kind of words are these to hear from
  Yellow Dog whom white man fears?

I take only what is mine, Lord, my pony,
  my squaw and my child,
I can't stay to see you die along with my tribe's
  pride.
I go to search for the yellow moon and the
  fathers of our sons
Where the red sun sinks in the hills of gold
  and the healing waters run.

Trampling down the prairie rose, leaving hoof
  tracks in the sand,
Those who wish to follow me I welcome with
  my hands.
I heard from passing renegades Geronimo was
  dead, he'd been
Laying down his weapons when they filled him
  full of lead.

Now there seems no reason why I should carry on
  in this land
That once was my land, I can't find a home.
It's lonely and it's quiet and the horse soldiers
  are coming
And I think it's time I strung my bow and ceased
  my senseless running.
For soon I'll find the yellow moon along with
  my loved ones,
Where the buffaloes graze in clover fields without
  the sound of guns.

And the red sun sinks at last into the hills of gold,
  and
Peace to this young warrior comes with a bullet
  hole.

HOLIDAY INN

Boston at last,
And the plane's touching down.
Our hostess is handing
The hot towels around.
From a terminal gate
To a black limousine,
It's a ten-minute ride
To the Holiday Inn.

Boredom's a pastime
That one soon acquired,
Where you get to the stage
Where you're not even tired;
Kicking your heels
Till the time comes around
To pick up your bags
And head out of town.

Slow down, Joe,
I'm a rock-'n-roll man,
I've twiddled my thumbs
In a dozen-odd bands;
And you ain't seen nothing
Until you've been in
A motel, baby,
Like the Holiday Inn.

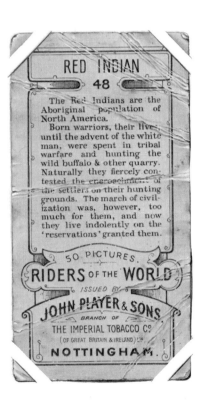

62

ALL THE NASTIES

If it came to pass
That they should ask,
What could I tell them?
Would they criticize
Behind my back?
Maybe I should let them.
Oh, if only then, and only then
They would understand,
They'd turn
A full-blooded city boy
Into a full blooded city man.

If they could face it,
I could take it,
In their eyes
I know I'd make it,
Their tiny minds
And sacred cows just fake it.
If only then, and only then
They would understand,
They'd turn
A full-blooded city boy
Into a full-blooded city man.

But I know the way
They want me,
In the way they publicize.
If they could turn
Their focus off
To the image in their eyes,
Maybe it would help them,
Help them understand
That a full-blooded city boy
Is now a full-blooded city man.

ROTTEN PEACHES

We've moved on six miles from where we were
    yesterday,
And yesterday is but a long, long ways away;
So we'll camp out tonight beneath the bright
    starlight,
And forget rotten peaches and the places we've
    stayed.

I left from the dockland two years ago now,
Made my way over on the S.S. *Marie*
And I've always had trouble wherever I've
    settled –
Rotten peaches are all that I see.

Rotten peaches rotting in the sun,
Seems I've seen that devil fruit since the world
    begun,
Mercy, I'm a criminal, Jesus, I'm the one –
Rotten peaches rotting in the sun.

There ain't no green grass in a U.S. state prison,
There is no one to hold when you're sick for your
    wife;
And each day out you'll pick, you'll pick rotten
    peaches,
You'll pick rotten peaches for the rest of your life.

Oh, I've had me fill of cocaine and pills,
For I lie in the light of the Lord,
And my home is ten thousand, ten thousand miles
    away,
And I guess I won't see it no more.

Rotten peaches rotting in the sun,
Seems I've seen that devil fruit since the world
    begun,
Mercy, I'm a criminal, Jesus, I'm the one –
Rotten peaches rotting in the sun.

63

Bernie Taupin was born
in Market Rasen Lincolnshire
and began writing poetry
at school. He now lives in a
nice cottage in the country
which he loves very much

THE GREATEST DISCOVERY

BIRTH

Peering out of tiny eyes,
The grubby hands that gripped the rail
Wiped the window clean of frost
As the morning air lay on the latch.

A whistle awakened someone there,
Next door to the nursery just down the hall:
A strange new sound he never heard before,
A strange new sound that makes boys explore.

Tread neat so small those little feet,
Amid the morning his small heart beats,
So much excitement yesterday
Must be rewarded, must be displayed.

Large hands lift him through the air,
Excited eyes contain him there,
The eyes of those he loves and knows,
But what's this extra bed just here?

His puzzled head tipped to one side,
Amazement swims in those bright green eyes,
Glancing down upon this thing
That makes strange sounds,
Strange sounds that sing.

In those silent happy seconds
That surround the sound of this event
A parent's smile is made in moments,
They have made for you a friend.

And all you ever learnt from them
Until you grew much older
Did not compare with when they said –
'This is your brand-new brother.'

Inside of you I have formed my home,
Outside of you I have cast a dome.
A castle you conceived for me,
This place to rest before I see.

All forms of life your band of love
Made me in silent hours,
Preparing I your destiny,
Your life, your time, your pride.

Beauty was beauty then;
For the spell of life had entered in
On a lifeline cord like holy word,
You are mine and I am yours.

For the journey is ending,
Your privileged pain is passing
Like a light in a window
At the end of a tunnel,
Out into the daytime,
From out of the night,
My darkness is over,
My whole world is light.

66

68

Though cowboys lived and died for fun.

END OF A DAY

Sweet the smell of burning wood
In coals the furnace formed its face,
Where infant eyes conceived much pleasure,
All dancing in the leaping opera.

Warm and wild the food of night
Takes hold, its charge deep down inside,
Around small frames late moments touch,
And love surrounds your cotton bunch.

Spread farewell on the dawning day,
A kiss that stemmed from every place,
Never to forget who sent him here,
His prayers for them are shed but never unaware.

A mountain conquered in grappling haste,
An island where the secrets stayed
Between the ones who sent him there,
And the pleas to read like a bedside chair.

Oh, Milne, for me a master mind,
Who walked in woods for every smile,
And took you with him every night
To keep your mind a neat concept, a worthy flight.

Small furry one the friend abode,
One eye gone and seams undone,
While fresh hands turn on passages
As eager as the smaller one.

The counterpane and night-light catch
Sides to be tucked in and reassured,
For every second means so much,
Perhaps more in his captain's tower.

Alone with shadows in his room,
Some tall and short in empty space,
No whisper for his thoughts induce,
When lids seal down and cease to move.

ROWSTON MANOR

You mighty manor built of stone
In the care of a county made to last,
Your lofty flints that laughed aloud
When I came one day to play a part,

Your compassion welled from deep inside,
Windows watched with ancient style,
A rustic monarch building pride
Had a deep effect on the country's child.

For the spinney rocked with poison bands
Made Robin Hood a worth-while game,
But crying cracked some sturdy plans
And timeless bliss was an endless game.

Near-Gothic was the place we ruled,
And the gargoyles charmed our lawn;
But a sponge cake ate on a windowsill
Marked when the new home was born.

You learn to know that a snowman cries
When the sun breaks out of the clouds;
And always pray there's a reason why
A butterfly's born in a shroud.

With Sheba chained tight to a chicken-run,
In small eyes seemed so absurd,
But life for her was a bundle of fun
As if Nania existed on earth.

The skyline spire peered down with ease,
A cricket-match with our family a-field,
While the silver birch reigned supreme king of
    trees,
Its secrets and senses unrevealed.

Though cowboys lived and died for fun,
The end was always so far ahead.
For a black cat fell foul to the farmer's gun
And the world was asleep in bed.

But the exit of the seasons shall fall
Like a dead leaf out of our lives.
We will leave this place with its secret walls
And its tell-tale heart deep inside.

69

TO A GRANDFATHER

Willow weep
Large tears of rain,
That fell through autumn skies
And took toll of time in silence,
When even the smallest thing cried
When one of the great living things died.

What more to ask,
When nature is born around you,
And all things growing grow for you,
And all things living live for you.

Some monuments
Time can never replace,
To rebuild an age
That will never be seen again.

But we will never cease to forget,
For as long as the storm of history books
Compels our lives,
There is only who haunts the corridors of time.

Who took two children,
Hand-in-hand down the lengthy lanes of
        Havrome,
Exploring things so long ago,
Like some misty memory from another land.

All the birds of the air
Flew the flags
And sang the hymns on a funeral day.
You say it was a sad day,
But it was still a day of sun,
A sun-day.

The earth was warm for taking,
For we were giving this to him,
A place to rest and be
In the garden of the cemetery,
Where life makes love to him,
And we will always always remember him.

FLATTERS
(A Beginning)

In furrows where the seagulls stole
The seed that was then sown by man,
To a rabbit hutch, and a milkman's bell
That rang by the gate and sang.

In duffel-coats and dirty socks,
The years had eyes in the sky that watched,
Surveyed them control the mighty machine,
Their scrap-metal island
Once a tractor had been;
Life forms from fields the elders had ploughed,
Where the crow and the kestrel
And the cormorant cried.

Naked and young the flesh that was born
Inside the left window,
Was a clown on the lawn;
And an odyssey was cast,
From the days that went last,
Where the sickle and scythe were as corn;
Hear the thunder of rocks
That shook through the elms,
Our community calls screamed the swarm
Of black hell.

72

Bernie Taupin The One Who Writes The Words For Elton John

CONCLUSION

Bracing up to face the wind I see him,
For he is one who will not weep
When his branches are bound together by
The manacles of the morning;
Here alone in pastoral settings,
Rigging the sails of my young palms
And turning towards the whistling barley,
Who plays much sweeter songs among her stalks
Then any classic
Strummed upon the sweetest of guitars.

For I shall grow,
My eyes will know,
Far into changes I must go,
To which in time I wasted once before,
Not knowing that my age was minor to my
Futuristic convictions.

Too early for the sunset,
I was born within four walls and
Neither of my faces
Could see the future far;
But some passages will be cruel,
For time has always been so,
But no day is so bright
Until it is graced by the call of the wild.

Only such a passage small as this
Can bear the brunt of things to come;
For as the days feed time's command,
I thank all those within whose
Arms I learnt to live and love
Their life for ever and ever
Until the end of time.

SOLITUDE

A strange obsession filled the stone
That ached in pleasure round this building,
As if deep within its age
A pounding heart was beating faster
Every moment I grew older.

No crevice was such as mine
That stooped beneath the holly hedges,
Kissed in lilac, roped in ivy;
This pleasure-ground of secret beauty,
Where summer's watchful eyes talked
And passers-by, silently tired, smiled.

Half-humid clouds passed by
Bleating playfully in the acres of the sky;
Sparrows bid a fond farewell
And buffeted among the elms,
The young world laughed and chased the breeze
Down tunnels trimmed in cobweb lace.

For Rory scowled,
Blazened bronze against the morning,
Peering between the rising fern,
And watching as I did
(For we shared what we had) and
The villagers continued by
Upon the crutches of our time.

BROTHERS TOGETHER

Amid the rocks that shone and sparkled,
Trout of sizes incomparable
Dived and danced in naked wonder
Along the crystal sparkling waters

While we three watched, wide eyes surveying
On warmer days when time was sparing,
For little did we realize how much we loved
The life we shared:
So short a time to build a dream,
But large enough to love that stream.

To watch the chestnut warriors,
Majestic towers of wooden wonder,
Bearing overwhelming gifts for all the
Children of the earth.

The sun burned down their old brown leaves,
And we kicked them and crushed them beneath
Our small feet.

Our first love was that shady glade,
For she always was a wondrous place.
But if only time could then secure my
Satisfied seclusion point,
Then every day I would walk across the old
Stone bridge down a woody path, and stare
Once more – old man and I – deep into the
Chalice of our lives where nature is the
Greatest thing, and the power of beauty
Is an everyday thing.

73

THE VISITOR

She sat in the captain's old rocking-chair
Lying in wait as the lights went out,
And the lamps in the street dimmed into
    darkness
As she rocked back and forth in her
    grandmother's house.

The seat creaked in the empty room
As her eyes flickered into life,
And they gazed full-length at the falling moon
And they cut through the stars like a knife.

And without full knowing her own tiny head
She walked to the ledge in a trance,
Where she eased off the latch,
Screamed at the sky
And suddenly started to dance.

But none of the dances you may know,
But one of a child possessed,
And as she danced her fingers clenched
And tore at the lace of her dress.

A candle flickered, no one stirred,
A smell of lavender strong,
As she spiralled on in her dance of death
And muttered an unholy song.

For soon her body became so willing
It sank in a heap on the floor
While a shadow floated into the room
And silently pushed to the door.

She sat in the captain's old rocking-chair
Lying in wait for the sun to come out,
And the morning to bring light to the hills
As she rocked back and forth
In her grandmother's house.

WHEN THE HERON WAKES

When the heron wakes
And sorrow leaves the lady of the river
And summer sings again,
Where wind kissed life and life blessed rain
By wild grass and windows
Where the fisherman was praying,

For I will be as the Valkyrie
With the strains of the war-dogs to leash,
Feeding their skulls in a feast of red sky,
Picking the pieces from all those who sin,
In the balm of a bright life
And a dead day by the sweet knife.

Captain Clegg has nothing on me,
Riding the pickets of wise Walter Small
Who is buried in Shamrock on top of the wolds.
Wise but a fool to walk through a wall
In front of the verger, the window and all
What a state but the bold community roars.

When the heron wakes
I'll resurrect the sparrow bones in life,
As once a child took a trowel.
Took a walk amongst the wild flowers,
Fell on his face and lay for hours,
I think the only time
He understands the world about.

76

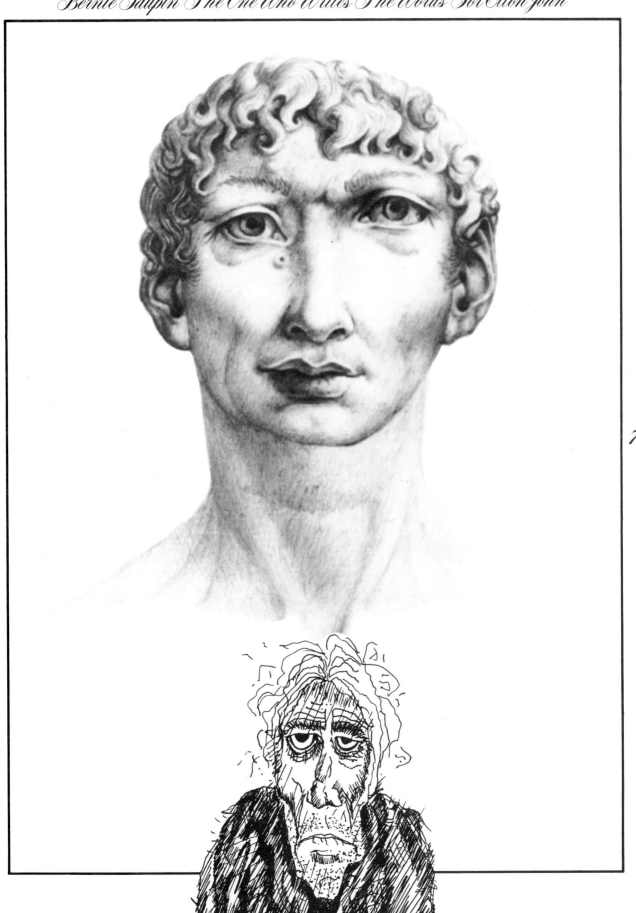

TODAY'S HERO

It was to breathe and give all the way,
With magic mixed in the eyes of the mad;
My human heart will doubtless decay.
Would the church spire topple beneath God's flag,
Am I really your hero today?

The clear broke into an endless well,
The grey walls sighed from the virgin cries;
Had he said, 'For your body my body repels –
Have I used you in the sun or the darkness skies?'
She had answered him lately saying –
'What else and why?'

But it was I who laughed, full of rum,
And kept all my friends in their sleep,
Such noted, a man could be left so undone,
For so many of his women were as sheep, and each
One in his company learned to bleat.

There's no one on the rooftop now,
While few sit close to the chequers set.
Cheating continued while all still allowed,
At the alms-house there's better still yet,
For that place and this I have no regret.

I've wasted in rain more than is my need,
I've cut off my wrists to be kind,
And I watch while my cuts freely bleed,
Flung out is the freedom of mind,
Martyred am I in a year of brown wine.

But I've entered where I've had to go,
Richer than a man who's dead;
Paying back the pool-rooms that I owe,
What can I say,
When most of it's been said?
The school-days and schoolgirls
I knew have fled.

SISTERS OF THE CROSS

The old gates are always locked
By the daughter of the keys,
Sad eyes are fixed upon the world
From the balcony.
While the six o'clock procession
Take their hymn-books to the hall,
It's sad to see them shed a tear
Inside the convent walls.

Red mountains around them
Keep out those who come,
But only birds and wild deer
Share the lives of nuns;
While ladies who in kindness
Burn the knowledge they have found,
Their knowledge lies inside a hole
Buried in the ground.

For the Sisters of the Cross
Seek the shadows they have lost,
In the walls where their lives
Are protected by God.
But the feeling of love
Is somewhere in your bones,
Your body is wasted
When it should have been owned.

The Mother of the mission bells
Has lived here all her life,
She never feels the hands of man
Touch her in the night;
And the canopies that cover her,
So cold and so afraid,
Thinking holy mothers die
Like spinsters in the grave.

To be single in the chapel
Praying knelt down on your knees,
Where corridors are echoing their proud
    solemnity;
And the candle-light against the glass
Plays shadow-chasing tricks,
As young girls fall, their eyes in tears,
Beside the crucifix.

79

LIKE SUMMER TEMPESTS

And now that it's all over,
The wings return to the feathered plume;
My mirror can reflect the moon, but somehow
I'm aware I think we arrived too soon.

Then, always then,
Introduced unknown to me
A living breath
To breathe beside still waters,
To crush the flower I never meant to alter.

But then again who knows?
Not I to wear the gospel
When I only wrote my own;
Your chapters shall go unwritten,
For I tried to show where I had grown, but
Now that mirror's broken, and I don't
Own you any more.

To hope for something better would be unkind;
The laziness I am goes far,
For I keep in my sake only you are fair,
And the web that was woven
For our peace of mind
Is lost in the rut of a man made kind.

LA PETITE MARIONETTE

I once was a marionette
Who danced in plays for children,
Who sang in a box with curtains on it
And cried in a trunk with chains around it.

I lay on an island of castaway ribbons,
With a cat and a dog that howled for light.
The dog's name was Dakri
And it fed on cold liver,
The cat's name was a number
And it died with the winter.

At Christmas shows in village halls
His hands would thrust inside me,
I screamed but no one heard me
My papier-mâché mouth sealed tightly.

I lived but no one believed me,
I loved but no one knew me,
And one day he up and he burned me,
For biting the hand
That manœuvred me.

RATCATCHER

I can't find a light in here,
I forgot to bring my torch and
It's very dark in there.
I can hear them moving round but
I can't see where,
I must exterminate, do my job and clear the air.
God, it's cold as hell in here.

I saw a pair of eyes
From a crack inside the wall,
Evil little points of fire
That make your backbone crawl,
And when you're down among their kind
You feel so bloody small,
Your throat's as dry as cardboard
And no one heeds a call.

If God's a friend of mine let me do my job and go.
I know they're all around me and they want me on
    my own,
But I'll have the last laugh on them when I take
Their corpses home and nail them to my garden
    shed
Till there's nothing left but bone.

But if only I could see them then I know that I'd
    be calm,
But God, how can I manage when I know they're
    all around,
How can I lay a bait when all I hear is their
    sound?
I know, I'll come back tomorrow when the
    light-switch can be found.

Yes, let's go and get some air, my eyes are getting
    sore.
I seem to see things now that I never saw before,
Grinning skulls and picked white bones upon the
    cold stone floor –
And Lord have mercy on me –
Someone's locked the door.

80

HONKY CAT

When I look back,
Boy, I must have been green,
Boppin' in the country,
Fishin' in a stream.

Lookin' for an answer,
Tryin' to find a sign,
Until I saw your city lights,
Honey, I was blind.

They said, 'Get back, Honky Cat,
Better get back to the woods,'
Well, I quit those days and my redneck ways,
And oh! oh! oh! oh! the change is gonna do me
    good.

'You better get back, Honky Cat,
Livin' in the city ain't where it's at;
It's like tryin' to find gold in a silver mine,
It's like tryin' to drink whiskey from a bottle of
    wine.'

Well, I read some books and I read some
    magazines,
About those high-class ladies
Down in New Orleans.
And all the folks back home said I was a fool,
They said, 'Believe in the Lord
Is the golden rule.'

They said, 'Stay at home, boy, you gotta tend
    the farm,
Livin' in the city, boy,
Is gonna break your heart.'
But how can you stay when your heart says no,
How can you stop
When your feet say go?

MELLOW

Cool grass blowin' up the pass, don't you know
    I'm feeling mellow?
I love your Roman nose, the way you curl your
    toes,
Baby, makes me feel so mellow.

It's the same old feelin' I get when you're
    stealin'
Back into my bed again,
With the curtains closed and the window froze
By the rhythm of the rain.

You make me mellow, you make me mellow,
Rockin' smooth and slow;
Mellow's the feeling that we get
Watchin' the coal fire glow.

You make me mellow, I make you mellow,
Wreckin' the sheets real fine;
Heaven knows what you sent me, Lord,
But God, this is a mellow time.

Going down to the stores in town, gettin' all the
    things we need,
Don't forget the beer, my little dear,
It helps to sow the mellow seed.

And it can't be bad,
All the love I've had
Coursin' through my life,
Down in the pass
Where the wind blows fast,
And mellow's a feelin' right.

Bernie Taupin The One Who Writes The Words For Elton John

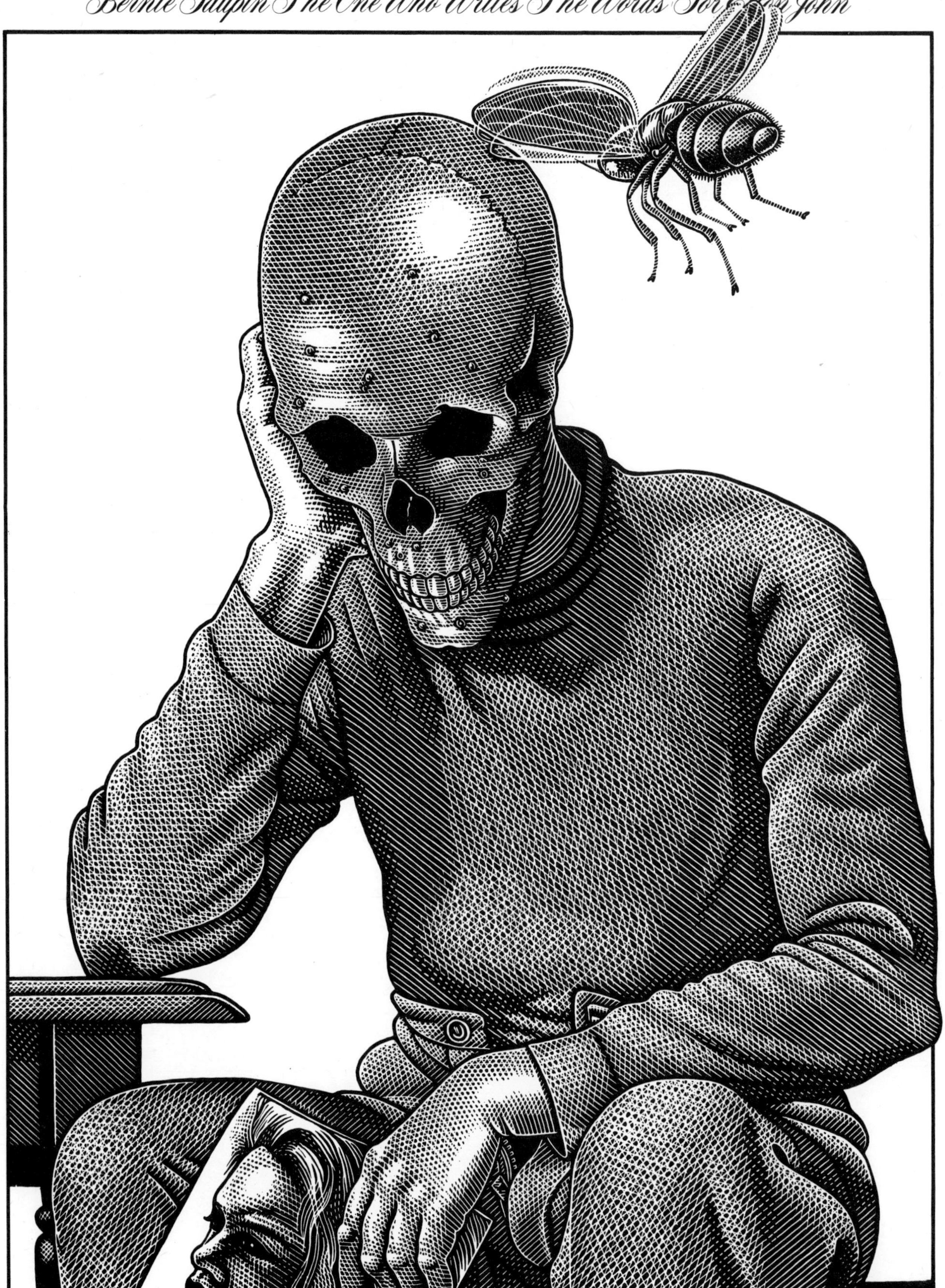

SUSIE
(Dramas)

I THINK I'M GOING TO KILL MYSELF

I got frost-bitten in the winter
Ice-skating on the river
With my pretty little black-eyed girl,
She'd make your darn toes curl
Just to see her.

I got a fringe front on my buggy,
I got a frisky little colt in a hurry
And a pretty little black-eyed Susie by my side.

Well, she sure knows how to use me,
Pretty little black-eyed Susie,
Playing hookey with my heart all the time;
Living with her funky family
In a derelict old alley
Down by the river where we share a little lovin' in
    the moonshine.

I'm an old hayseed harp-player,
I'm the hit of the county fair,
With my pretty little black-eyed girl
Living proof as she swirls –
She's a dancer.

I'm getting bored
Being part of mankind,
There's not a lot to do no more,
This race is a waste of time.

People rushing everywhere,
Swarming round like flies;
Think I'll buy a forty-four,
Give 'em all a surprise.

Think I'm gonna kill myself,
Cause a little suicide,
Stick around for a couple of days –
What a scandal if I died!

Yeah, I'm gonna kill myself,
Get a little headline news,
I'd like to see what the papers say
On the state of teenage blues.

A rift in my family,
I can't use the car,
I gotta be in by ten o'clock –
Who do they think they are?

I'd make an exception
If you want to save my life,
Brigitte Bardot's gotta come
And see me every night.

87

ROCKET MAN
(I think it's going to be a long, long time)

She packed my bags last night
Pre-flight,
Zero hour nine a.m.
And I'm gonna be high as a kite by then.

I miss the earth so much,
I miss my wife,
It's lonely out in space
On such a timeless flight.

And I think it's gonna be a long, long time
Till touch-down brings me round again to find
I'm not the man they think I am at home;
Oh! no, no, no,
I'm a rocket man,
Rocket man burning out his fuse up here alone.

Mars ain't the kind of place to raise your kids,
In fact it's cold as hell,
And there's no one there to raise them if you did.

And all this science
I don't understand,
It's just my job five days a week –
A rocket man.

SALVATION

I have to say, my friends,
This road goes a long, long way,
And if we're going to find the end
We're gonna need a helping hand.

I have to say, my friends,
We're looking for a light ahead,
In the distance a candle burns,
Salvation keeps the hungry children fed.

It's gotta take a lot of salvation,
What we need are willing hands;
You must feel the sweat in your eyes,
You must understand salvation.

A chance to put the devil down
Without the fear of hell,
Salvation spreads the gospel round
And frees you from yourself.

89

90

SLAVE

There's a river running sweat right through our
   land,
Driven by a man with a bullwhip in his hand,
And I've taken just as much as I can stand,
Oh, we've got to free our brothers from their
   shackles if we can.

Most nights I have to watch my woman cry,
Every day I watch the colonel smile,
His painted ladies riding in from town,
I swear one day I'm gonna burn that whore-house
   to the ground.

Slave! Slave!
To fight the violence we must brave,
Hold on strong
To the love God gave slave.

There's a rumour of a war that's yet to come
That may free our families and our sons;
It may lay green lands to barren wastes,
The price of release is a bitter blow to face.

AMY

Tread on my face if you like, little lady,
Turn me inside out if you have to, baby,
But don't you cross me off your list,
I am young and I ain't never been kissed,
Never been kissed by a lady called Amy.

You're far out, you're fab and insane,
A woman of the world, it's quite plain,
My dad told me Amy's your name,
Said he'd break my neck if I played your game,
But he can bust my neck, 'cause I love you all the
   same.

Amy, I know you don't have to show your
   affection,
'Cause the big boys like you and to you I'm an
   infection,
So if you don't want me around
I think I'll run along and drown,
You can't want this bum in town, Amy.

I'm beaten on the streets 'cause I loves you,
I watch you go to work in the summer,
I don't whistle at you down the street –
I would if I could, but I can't whistle, you see.

Amy, I may not be James Dean,
Amy, I may not be nineteen,
And I may still be in romper boots and jeans,
But Amy, you're the girl that wrecks my dreams.

MONA LISAS AND MAD HATTERS

HERCULES

92

And now I know Spanish Harlem
Are not just pretty words to say,
I thought I knew,
But now I know that rose-trees never grow
In New York City.

Until you've seen this trash-can dream come true,
You stand at the edge while people run you
 through,
And I thank the Lord there's people out there
 like you.

While Mona Lisas and Mad Hatters,
Sons of bankers, sons of lawyers,
Turn around and say good morning to the night,
For unless they see the sky,
But they can't and that is why
They know not if it's dark outside or light.

This Broadway's got a lot of songs to sing,
If I knew the tunes I might join in;
I'll go my way alone,
Grow my own, my own seeds shall be sown
In New York City.

Subway's no way for a good man to go down,
Rich man can ride and the hobo he can drown,
And I thank the Lord for the people I have found.

Ooh! I got a busted wing,
And a hornet sting
Like an out-of-tune guitar,
Oh! she got Hercules on her side
And Diana in her eyes.

Some men like the Chinese life,
Some men kneel and pray,
Well, I like women,
And I like wine,
And I've always liked it that way,
Always liked it that way.

But I can't dig it,
The way she tease.
That old tough man routine up her sleeve,
Livin' and a lovin', kissin' and a huggin',
Livin' and a lovin' with a cat named Hercules.

Oh! and it hurts like hell
To see my gal
Messin' with a muscle boy,
No superman gonna ruin my plans
Playin' with my toys.

Rich man sweatin' in a sauna bath,
Poor boy scrubbin' in a tub,
Me I stay gritty up to my ears
Washing in a bucket of mud,
Washing in a bucket of mud.

DANIEL

Daniel is travelling tonight on a plane,
I can see the red tail-lights heading for Spain;
Oh, and I can see Daniel waving goodbye,
God, it looks like Daniel, must be the clouds in
    my eyes.

They say Spain is pretty, though I've never been,
Well, Daniel says it's the best place he's ever seen,
Oh, and he should know, he's been there enough,
Lord, I miss Daniel, oh, I miss him so much.

Oh, Daniel, my brother,
You are older than me,
Do you still feel the pain
Of the scars that won't heal?
Your eyes have died, but you see more than I,
Daniel, you're a star in the face of the sky.

TEACHER, I NEED YOU

I was sitting in the class-room
Trying to look intelligent
In case the teacher looked at me.
She was long and she was lean,
She's a middle-aged dream
And that lady means the whole world to me.

It's a natural achievement
Conquering my homework
With her image pounding in my brain.
She's an inspiration
For my graduation
And she helps to keep the class-room sane.

Oh, teacher, I need you
Like a little child,
You got something in you
To drive a schoolboy wild.

You give me education
In the lovesick blues,
Help me get straight, come out and say –
Teacher, I – Teacher, I – Teacher, I –
Teacher, I need you!

I have to write a letter,
Tell about my feelings
Just to let her know the scene.
Focus my attention
On some further education
In connection with the birdies and the bees.

So I'm sitting in the class-room,
I'm looking like a zombie,
I'm waiting for the bell to ring.
I've got John Wayne stances,
I've got Erroll Flynn advances
And it doesn't mean a doggone thing.

ELDERBERRY WINE

There's a fly in the window, a dog in the yard,
And a year since I saw you;
There's a trunk in the corner I keep all my letters,
My bills and demands I keep too.

But I can't help thinkin' about the times
You were a wife of mine;
You aimed to please me, cooked blacked-eyed
     peas-me,
Made Elderberry Wine.

Drunk all the time, feelin' fine
On Elderberry Wine,
Those were the days, we'd lie in the haze
Forget depressive times.

How can I ever get it together
Without a wife in line
To pick the crop and get me hot
On Elderberry Wine?

Round a tree in the summer, a fire in the fall,
Flat out when we couldn't stand,
The bottle went round like a woman down South
Passed on from hand to hand.

But I can't help thinkin' about the times
You were a wife of mine,
You aimed to please me, cooked blacked-eyed
     peas-me,
Made Elderberry Wine.

BLUES FOR BABY AND ME

Your old man got mad when I told him we were
     leaving,
He cursed and he raged and he swore at the
     ceiling,
He called you his child, said 'Honey, get wise to
     his game,
He'll get you in trouble, I know it, those bums are
     all the same.'
There's a Greyhound outside in the lane,
     it's waiting for us,
So tell him goodbye, we gotta go west on that bus.

And it's all over now,
Don't you worry no more,
Gonna go west to the sea;
The Greyhound is swaying
And the radio's playing
Some blues for baby and me.
And the highway looks like it never did,
Lord, it looks so sweet and so free,
And I can't forget that trip to the west,
Singing blues for baby and me.

Saw your hands trembling, your eyes opened in
     surprise,
It's ninety in the shade, babe, and there ain't a
     cloud in the sky.
I called you my child, said 'Honey, now this is
     our game,
There's two of us to play it, and I'm happy to be
     home again.'
There's a Greyhound outside in the lane,
     it's waiting for us,
So tell him goodbye, we gotta go west on that bus.

99

MIDNIGHT CREEPER

Walk a mile in my tennis shoes,
Tina Turner gave me the highway blues,
But I don't love nobody but you, honey.

I'm true rat for the things I done,
Second cousin to a son of a gun,
I'm gonna wipe out your mama if she puts me on,
    honey.

'Cause I'm a midnight creeper,
Ain't gonna lose no sleep over you.
When there's a nightmare, I'm there,
Tempting you to blow a fuse.

Well, there's no more sleepin'
When I'm midnight creepin' over you,
Watch out, honey, watch out, honey,
Watch the things you do.

Long-haired ladies, well they look so fine
Locked in my cellar full of cheap red wine,
But I don't think those ladies, they really mind,
    honey.

I still don't know why you hate me so,
A little bit of fun never stopped no show,
Well, I just want to loosen up my soul, honey.

HAVE MERCY ON THE CRIMINAL

Have you heard the dogs at night
Somewhere on the hill,
Chasing some poor criminal,
And I guess they're out to kill?
Oh, there must be shackles on his feet
And Mother in his eyes, stumbling through the
    devil-dark
With the hound pack in full cry –

Have mercy on the criminal
Who is running from the law,
Are you blind to the
Winds of change,
Don't you hear him any more?

Praying, 'Lord, you gotta help me,
I am never gonna sin again,
Just take these chains
From around my legs,
Sweet Jesus, I'll be your friend.'

Now have you ever seen
The white teeth gleam
While you lie on a
Cold damp ground?
You're taking in the face of a rifle butt
While the wardens hold you down,
And you've never seen a friend in years.
Oh, it turns your heart to stone,
You jump the walls,
And the dogs run free,
And the grave's gonna be your home.

100

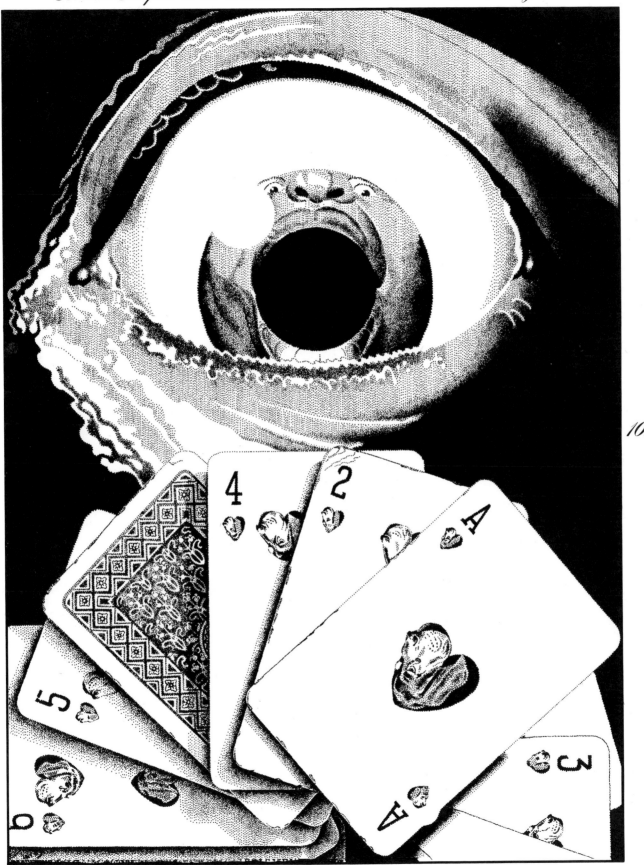

I'M GOING TO BE A TEENAGE IDOL

Well, there's slim times when my words
    won't rhyme,
And the hills I face are a long hard climb,
I just sit cross-legged with my old guitar,
Ooh! it kind of makes me feel like a rock-and-roll
    star.

Well, it makes me laugh, Lord, it makes me cry,
And I think for once, let me just get high,
Let me get electric, put a silk suit on,
Turn my old guitar into a tommy-gun.

And root, toot, shoot myself to fame,
Every kid alive gonna know my name,
An overnight phenomenon like there's never been,
A motivated supersonic king of the scene.

I'll be a teenage idol, just give me a break,
I'm gonna be a teenage idol, no matter how long
    it takes.
You can't imagine what it means to me,
I'm gonna grab myself a place in history,
A teenage idol, that's what I'm gonna be.

Well, life is short and the world is rough,
And if you're gonna boogie, boy, you gotta be
    tough.
Nobody knows if I'm dead or alive,
I just drink myself to sleep each night.

And so I pray to the teenage god of rock,
If I make it big, let me stay on top,
You gotta cut me loose from this one-room dive,
Put me on the ladder, keep this boy alive.

TEXAN LOVE SONG

I heard from a friend you'd been messin' around
With a cute little thing I'd been dating uptown;
Well, I don't know if I like that idea much,
Well, you'd better stay clear, I might start
    acting rough.

You out-of-town guys sure think you're real keen,
Think all of us boys here are homespun and green;
But that's wrong, my friend, so get this through
    your head,
We're tough and we're Texan with necks good
    and red.

So it's Ki-i-yippie-yi-yi,
You long-hairs are sure gonna die,
Our American home was clean till you came,
And kids still respected the president's name.

And the eagle still flew in the sky,
Hearts filled with national pride.
Then you came along with your drug-crazy
    songs –
Goddammit, you're all gonna die.

How dare you sit there and drink all our beer,
Oh, it's made for us workers who sweat, spit and
    swear,
The minds of our daughters are poisoned by you,
With your communistic politics and them
    Negro blues.

Well, I'm gonna quit talking and take action now,
Run all of you fairies clean out of this town,
Oh, I'm dog-tired of watchin' you mess up our
    lives,
Spending the summertime naturally high.

CROCODILE ROCK

I remember when rock was young,
Me and Susie had so much fun,
Holdin' hands and skimmin' stones,
Had an old gold Chevy and a place of my own.

But the biggest kick I ever got
Was doing a thing called the Crocodile Rock;
While the other kids were rockin' round the clock,
We were hoppin' and boppin' to the Crocodile
    Rock.

Well, Crocodile Rockin' is something shockin',
When your feet just can't keep still;
I never knew me a better time,
And I guess I never will.

Oh, lawdy mama, those Friday nights,
When Susie wore her dresses tight,
And the Crocodile Rockin' was out of sight.

But the years went by and rock just died,
Susie went and left me for some foreign guy;
Long nights cryin' by the record machine,
Dreamin' of my Chevy and my old blue jeans.

But they'll never kill the thrills we've got,
Burnin' up to the Crocodile Rock,
Learnin' fast as the weeks went past,
We really thought the Crocodile Rock would last.

HIGH-FLYING BIRD

You wore a little cross of gold around your neck,
I saw it as you flew between my reason,
Like a raven in the night-time when you left;
I wear a chain upon my wrist that bears no name,
You touched it and you wore it,
And you kept it in your pillow all the same.

My high-flying bird has flown from out my arms,
I thought myself her keeper,
She thought I meant her harm,
She thought I was the archer,
A weather-man of words,
But I could never shoot down
My high-flying bird.

The white walls of your dressing-room are
    stained in scarlet red,
You bled upon the cold stone like a young man
In the foreign field of death.
'Wouldn't it be wonderful?' is all I heard you say,
You never closed your eyes at night, and learned
    to love daylight –
Instead you moved away.

104

105

LOVE LIES BLEEDING

The roses in the window-box
Have tilted to one side,
Everything about this house
Was born to grow and die.

It doesn't seem a year ago
To this very day,
You said, 'I'm sorry, honey,
If I don't change the pace
I can't face another day.'

And love lies bleeding in my hand,
It kills me to think of you with another man:
I was playing rock-'n-roll and you were just a fan,
But my guitar couldn't hold you,
So I split the band;
Love lies bleeding in my hands.

I wonder if those changes
Have left a scar on you,
Like all the burning hoops of fire
That you and I passed through?

You're a bluebird on a telegraph line,
I hope you're happy now;
Well, if the wind of change comes down your way,
    girl,
You'll make it back somehow.

GOODBYE, NORMA JEAN

Goodbye, Norma Jean,
Though I never knew you at all;
You had the grace to hold yourself
While those around you crawled;
They crawled out of the woodwork,
And they whispered into your brain,
They set you on the treadmill,
And they made you change your name.

And it seems to me you lived your life
Like a candle in the wind,
Never knowing who to cling to
When the rain set in.
And I would have liked to have known you,
But I was just a kid,
Your candle burned out long before
Your legend ever did.

Loneliness was tough,
The toughest role you ever played;
Hollywood created a superstar –
And pain was the price you paid;
Even when you died,
The press still hounded you –
All the papers had to say
Was that Marilyn was found in the nude.

Goodbye, Norma Jean,
Though I never knew you at all;
You had the grace to hold yourself
While those around you crawled.

Goodbye, Norma Jean,
From the young man in the twenty-second row,
Who sees you as something more than sexual,
More than just our Marilyn Monroe.

"Candle in the wind"   Peter Blake. 1975.

110

BENNIE AND THE JETS

Hey, kids! Shake it loose together,
The spotlight's hitting something
That's been known to change the weather;
We'll kill the fatted calf tonight –
So stick around,
You're gonna hear electric music,
Solid walls of sound.

Say, Candy and Ronnie, have you seen them yet?
Wow! but they're so spaced out, Bennie and the
        Jets –
Oh! but they're weird and they're wonderful,
Oh! Bennie, she's really keen,
She's got electric boots, a mohair suit,
You know, I read it in a magazine,
Oh! Bennie and the Jets.

Hey, kids! Plug in to the faithless,
Maybe they're blinded,
But Bennie makes them ageless.
We shall survive, let us take ourselves along
Where we fight our parents out in the streets
To find who's right and who's wrong.

GOODBYE, YELLOW BRICK ROAD

When are you gonna come down?
When are you going to land?
I should have stayed on the farm–
I should have listened to my old man.

You know you can't hold me for ever,
I didn't sign up with you;
I'm not a present for your friends to open,
This boy's too young to be singing the blues.

So goodbye, yellow brick road,
Where the dogs of society howl;
You can't plant me in your penthouse,
I'm going back to my plough.

Back to the howling old owl in the woods,
Hunting the horny-back toad;
Oh, I've finally decided my future lies
Beyond the yellow brick road.

What do you think you'll do then?
I bet that'll shoot down your plane;
It'll take you a couple of vodka and tonics
To set you on your feet again.

Maybe you'll get a replacement,
There's plenty like me to be found;
Mongrels who ain't got a penny
Sniffing for tit-bits like you on the ground.

111

THIS SONG HAS NO TITLE

Tune me in to the wild side of life,
I'm an innocent young child sharp as a knife;
Take me to the garrets where the artists have died,
Show me the courtrooms where the judges have
    lied.

Let me drink deeply from the water and the wine,
Light coloured candles in dark dreary mines;
Look in the mirror and stare at myself,
And wonder if that's really me on the shelf.

And each day I learn just a little bit more,
I don't know why, but I do know what for;
If we're all going somewhere, let's get there soon,
This song's got no title, just words and a tune.

Take me down alleys where the murders are done,
In a vast high-powered rocket to the core of the
    sun;
I want to read books in the studies of men
Who are born on the breeze and die on the wind.

If I was an artist who paints with his eyes,
I'd study my subject and silently cry,
Cry for the darkness to come down on me,
For confusion to carry on turning the wheel.

GREY SEAL

Why's it never light on my lawn,
Why does it rain and never say good-day to the
    new-born?
On the big screen they showed us a sun,
But not as bright in life as the real one,
It's never quite the same as the real one.

And tell me, grey seal,
How does it feel
To be so wise,
To see through eyes
That only see what's real?
Tell me, grey seal.

I never learned why meteors were formed,
I only farmed in schools that were so worn and
    torn;
If anyone can cry then so can I,
I read books and draw life from the eye,
All my life is drawings from the eye.

Your mission bells were wrought by ancient men,
The roots were formed by twisted roots, your
    roots were twisted then;
I was reborn before all life could die,
The Phoenix bird will leave this world to fly,
If the Phoenix bird can fly, then so can I.

113

114

I'VE SEEN THAT MOVIE TOO

I can see by your eyes you must be lying
When you think I don't have a clue,
Baby, you're crazy
If you think that you can fool me,
Because I've seen that movie too.

The one where the players are acting surprised,
Saying love's just a four-letter word,
Between forcing smiles with the knives in their
    eyes,
Well, their actions become so absurd.

So keep your auditions for somebody
Who hasn't got so much to lose,
'Cause you can tell by the lines I'm reciting
That I've seen that movie too.

It's a habit I have, I don't get pushed around,
Stop twinkling your star like you do,
I'm not the blue-print
For all of your B films
Because I've seen that movie too.

JAMAICA JERK-OFF

When she gets up in the morning
It's enough to wake the dead,
Oh, she's turning on the radio
And dancing on my head.

It's no good living in the sun,
Playing guitar all day,
Boogalooin' with my friends
In that erotic way.

Come on, Jamaica!
In Jamaica all day,
Dancing with your darling,
Do Jamaica jerk-off that way.

Come on, Jamaica!
Everybody say
We're all happy in Jamaica,
Do Jamaica jerk-off that way.

Let the ladies and the gentlemen
Be as rude as they like,
On the beaches, oh, in the jungle,
Where the people feel all right.

So do it in Jamaica,
Got plenty for you and me,
Honky-tonkin' with my baby
In the deep blue sea.

THE BALLAD OF DANNY BAILEY (1909-34)   **DIRTY LITTLE GIRL**

Some punk with a shotgun
Killed young Danny Bailey
In cold blood in the lobby
Of a downtown motel.

Killed him in anger,
A force he couldn't handle
Helped pull the trigger
That cut short his life.

And there's not many knew him
The way that we did,
Sure enough he was a wild one
But then aren't most hungry kids?

Now it's all over, Danny Bailey,
And the harvest is in;
Dillinger's dead –
I guess the cops won again.
Now it's all over, Danny Bailey,
And the harvest is in.

We're running short of heroes
Back up here in the hills;
Without Danny Bailey
We're gonna have to break up our stills.

So mark his grave well,
'Cause Kentucky loved him;
Born and raised a pauper,
I guess life just bugged him.

And he found faith in danger,
A life-style he lived by,
A runnin' gun youngster
In a sad restless age.

I've seen a lot of women who haven't had much
    luck,
I've seen you looking like you've been run down
    by a truck;
That ain't nice to say, sometimes I guess I'm
    really hard,
But I'm gonna put buckshot in your pants if you
    step into my yard.

When I watch the police come by and move you
    on,
Well, I sometimes wonder what's beneath the
    mess you've become;
Well, you may have been a pioneer in the trade of
    women's wear,
But all you got was a mop-up job washing other
    people's stairs.

I'm gonna tell the world you're a dirty little girl,
Someone grab that bitch by the ears:
Rub her down, scrub her back,
And turn her inside out,
'Cause I bet she hasn't had a bath in years.

Here's my own belief about all the dirty girls –
That you have to clean the oyster to find the pearl;
And like rags that belong to you, I belong to
    myself,
So don't show up round here till your social
    worker's helped.

116

SWEET PAINTED LADY

I'm back on dry land once again,
Opportunity awaits me like a rat in a drain;
We're all hunting honey with money to burn,
Just a short time to show you the tricks that
    we've learned.

If the boys all behave themselves here,
Well, there's pretty young ladies and beer in the
    rear;
You won't need a gutter to sleep in tonight,
The prices I charge here will see you all right.

So she lays down beside me again,
My sweet painted lady, the one with no name;
Many have used her, and many still do,
There's a place in the world for a woman like you.

Oh, sweet painted lady,
Seems it's always been the same,
Getting paid for being laid,
Guess that's the name of the game.

Forget us, we'll have gone very soon,
Just forget we ever slept in your rooms;
And we'll leave the smell of the sea in your beds
Where love's just a job and nothing is said.

ALL THE GIRLS LOVE ALICE

Raised to be a lady by the golden rule,
Alice was the spawn of a public school,
With a double-barrel name in the back of her
    brain,
And a simple case of Mummy doesn't love me
    blues.

Reality it seems was just a dream,
She couldn't get it on with the boys on the scene,
But what do you expect from a chick who's just
    sixteen?
And hey, hey, hey, you know what I mean.

All the young girls love Alice;
Tender young Alice, they say –
Come over and see me,
Come over and please me,
Alice, it's my turn today.

All the young girls love Alice;
Tender young Alice, they say –
If I give you my number
Will you promise to call me?
Wait till my husband's away.

Poor little darling with a chip out of her heart,
It's like acting in a movie when you've got the
    wrong part;
Getting your kicks in another girl's bed,
And it was only last Tuesday they found you in
    the subway – dead.

And who could call your friends down in Soho?
One or two middle-aged dykes in a go-go –
And what do you expect from a sixteen-year-old
    yo-yo?
And hey, hey, hey,
Oh! don't you know?

119

SATURDAY NIGHT'S ALL RIGHT
FOR FIGHTING

It's gettin' late, have yer seen my mates?
Ma, tell me when the boys get here,
It's seven o'clock, and I want to rock,
Wanna get a belly full of beer.

My old man's drunker than a barrel full of
    monkeys,
And my old lady, she don't care,
My sister looks cute in her braces and boots,
A handful of grease in her hair.

So don't give us none of yer aggravation,
We've had it with yer discipline;
Saturday night's all right for fightin',
Get a little action in.

Get about as oiled as a diesel train,
Gonna set this dance alight,
'Cause Saturday night's the night I like,
Saturday night's all right, all right, all right.

Well, they're packed pretty tight in here tonight,
I'm looking for a dolly who'll see me right,
I may use a little muscle to get what I need,
I may sink a little drink and shout out 'She's
    with me.'

A couple of the sounds that I really like
Are the sound of a switchblade and a motorbike;
I'm a juvenile product of the working class,
Whose best friend floats in the bottom of a glass.

YOUR SISTER CAN'T TWIST
(But She Can Rock 'n' Roll)

I could really get off being in your shoes,
I used to be stone-sold on rhythm and blues,
I heard of a place at the back of town
Where you really kick shit when the sun goes
    down.

I really got buzzed when your sister said –
'Throw away them records 'cause the blues is
    dead,
Let me take you, honey, where the scene's on
    fire,'
And tonight I learned for certain that the blues
    expired.

Oh, your sister can't twist, but she can rock and
    roll,
Out-bucks the broncos in the rodeo-do,
She's only sixteen but it's plain to see
She can pull the wool over little old me;
Your sister can't twist, but she can rock and roll,
Your sister can't twist, but she got more soul
    than me.

Somebody help me 'cause the bug bit me,
Now I'm in heaven with the aching feet,
But I'll be back tonight where the music plays
And your sister rocks all my blues away.

120

122

ROY ROGERS

Sometimes you dream,
Sometimes it seems
There's nothing there at all;
You just seem older than yesterday,
And you're waiting for tomorrow to call.

You draw to the curtains,
And one thing's for certain,
You're cosy in your little room,
The carpet's all paid for,
God bless the TV,
Let's go shoot a hole in the moon.

And Roy Rogers is riding tonight,
Returning to our silver screens –
Comic-book characters never grow old,
Evergreen heroes whose stories were told –
The great sequin cowboy
Who sings of the plains,
Of round-ups and rustlers
And home on the range.
Turn on the TV,
Shut out the lights –
Roy Rogers is riding tonight.

Nine o'clock mornings,
Five o'clock evenings,
I'd liven the pace if I could;
I'd rather have ham in my sandwich than cheese,
But complaining wouldn't do any good.

Lay back in my armchair,
Close eyes and think clear,
I can hear hoofbeats ahead;
Roy and Trigger have just hit the hilltop,
While the wife and the kids are in bed.

SOCIAL DISEASE

My bulldog is barking in the back yard
Enough to raise a dead man from his grave;
And I can't concentrate on what I'm doing,
Disturbance going to crucify my days.

And the days they get longer and longer,
And the night-time is a time of little use;
For I just get ugly and older,
I get juiced on Mateus and just hang loose.

And I get bombed for breakfast in the morning,
I get bombed for dinner-time and tea;
I dress in rags, smell a lot, and have a real good
    time,
I'm a genuine example of a social disease.

My landlady lives in a caravan,
Well, that is when she isn't in my arms,
And it seems I pay the rent in human kindness,
But my liquor also helps to grease her palm.

And the ladies are all getting wrinkles
And they're falling apart at the seams,
While I just get high on tequila
And see visions of vineyards in my dreams.

HARMONY

Hello, baby, hello,
Haven't seen your face for a while;
Have you quit doing time for me,
Or are you still the same spoilt child?

Hello, I said hello,
Is this the only place you thought to go?
Am I the only man you ever had,
Or am I just the last surviving friend that you
    know?

Harmony and me
We're pretty good company;
Looking for an island
In our boat upon the sea.
Harmony, gee I really love you,
And I want to love you for ever
And dream of the never, never, never leaving
    Harmony.

Hello, baby, hello,
Open up your heart and let your feelings flow;
You're not unlucky knowing me,
Keeping the speed real slow;
In any case I set my own pace
By stealing the show, say hello, hello.

123

I am quite

at home at

A5150

time to write

ALL ACROSS THE HAVENS

The sister of sunlight
Comes to my lonely life,
Bearing the crosses I hung –
I hung on my lonely wife.

And the anchor told me,
If I prayed by the river,
That the sweet sound of water
Would always go with her.

All across the Havens
To the waterfall,
They told me I would meet her there
Inside those icy walls.

But how on earth
In this universe
Can they forgive me of my pains,
For all across the Havens
I must stumble,
Locked in chains.

Then the mother of mercy
Showed me her stable,
And told me you would be safe,
Safe in her cradle.

And the waterfall opened,
And the water withdrew,
Leaving me standing
On a road leading through.

JUST LIKE STRANGE RAIN

I looked up from my glass
Into the sky,
There's no room in my comic book to hide.
The calendar swung on the wall
Held by a rusty nail,
And down came the strange rain
And washed my thoughts away.

So stop in the sky and tell me why
You're changing your colours before my eyes;
Yellow, blue, green and grey
Settled on my window-pane,
And made the rain that came seem strange,
Just like strange rain.

And still I sat beside the fire,
And watched it as it fell,
Coming colours from above
Into my citadel.
My eyes are all embroidered
In the rainbow you have made,
Now it seems as though it's just,
Just like strange rain.

126

128

BAD SIDE OF THE MOON

It seems as though I've lived my life
On the bad side of the moon;
To stir your dregs in sickness still
Without the rustic spoon.

Common people live with me
Where the light has never shone,
And the hermits flock like hummingbirds
To speak in a foreign tongue.

I'm a lightyear away
From the people who make me stay
Sitting on the bad side of the moon.

There ain't no use for watchdogs here
To justify our ways,
We live our lives in manacles,
The main cause of our stay.

Exiled here from other worlds,
Our sentence comes too soon;
Why should I be made to pay
On the bad side of the moon?

LET ME BE YOUR CAR

I may not seem your ideal when you look into my
    eyes,
I don't smoke, I don't tell jokes, I'm not the
    custom-made size:
But baby, let me take you on the highway for a
    while,
I'll show you where the man in me is when he
    doesn't hide,
He's cruisin' in the fast lane,
Stuck behind the wheel,
Jekyll and Hyde going on inside
When I'm your automobile.

And let me be your car for a while, child,
Shift me into gear and I'll be there,
Fill me up with five-star gasoline,
I'll be your car, I'll take you anywhere.

I can't dance, I don't dig it, I can't see it at all,
You say I'm just a specimen, and baby, I can
    crawl,
My physique don't look the way physiques really
    should,
But then again I've got an engine underneath
    my hood.
When I'm cutting up the road
With a sports car on my tail,
Frankenstein's inside my mind
And the wind's inside my sails.

129

WHENEVER YOU'RE READY
(We'll Go Steady Again)

I lived in a tenement six floors above,
I lent you my records and I lent you my love,
But you left me on the weekend without a
    by-your-leave,
That's a dirty and a low-down trick, my folks all
    think you're mean.

But I don't mind, that's kind of nifty,
You always see those break-ups in the movies;
And just like a light you put me out,
Now I'm gonna do my best
To get you back in the nest you came from.

You can erase me if you want to,
Turn your sights on other men,
But whenever you're ready,
Honey, we'll go steady again.

It's nasty without you in my little room,
I miss you like crazy, please come back soon;
I was joking with those things I said,
I couldn't have been thinking,
If you don't come back I think I'll crack,
Just like my old ceiling.

INTO THE OLD MAN'S SHOES

I'm moving out of Tombstone
With the sun behind my back,
I'm tired of people talking
Of the things that I did lack.
Ever since a week ago,
The day he passed away,
I've been taking too much notice
Of the things they've had to say.

And all they say
Is – you ain't half the man he used to be,
He had strength and worked his life
To feed his family.
So if that's the way it has to be,
I'll say goodbye to you,
I'm not the guy, or so it seems,
To fill my old man's shoes.

Like I'm a wicked way of life,
The kind that must be tamed,
They'd like to see me locked in jail
And tied up in their chains.
Oh! It's hard, and I can't see
What they want me to do, Lord,
They seem to think
I should step into my old man's shoes.

STEP INTO CHRISTMAS

Welcome to my Christmas song,
I'd like to thank you for the year.
So I'm a-sending you this Christmas card
To say it's nice to have you here.

I'd like to sing about all the things
Your eyes and mine can see,
So hop aboard your turn-table
Oh, step into Christmas with me, yeah.

Step into Christmas, let's join together,
We can watch the snow fall for ever and ever,
Eat, drink and be merry, come along with me,
Step into Christmas, the admission's free.

Take care in all you do next year
And keep smiling through the days.
If we can help to entertain you,
Oh, we will find the ways.

So merry Christmas, one and all,
There's no place I'd rather be
Than asking you if you'll oblige
Stepping into Christmas with me.

Step into Christmas, let's join together,
We can watch the snow fall for ever and ever,
Eat, drink and be merry, come along with me
Step into Christmas, the admission's free.

130

132

SCREW YOU

When I was a boy I had a lot of fun,
I lived by the sea, I was a fisherman's son;
My mother, she was a fisherman's wife,
She was scrubbing floors most of her life.

They said, Screw you,
I ain't got nothing to lose,
I could paper a matchbox
With the money I use.

At the school I attended I got into fights,
I was beaten in an alley on a cold winter night;
The teachers cared less for the blood in our veins,
They got most of their thrills out of using the cane.

They said, Screw you,
Oh, you bloody young fools,
I could get more sense out of the back end of a
    mule.

So you see, there's men who get paid for being
    slaves,
And men who get paid for being free,
And there's men behind bars who pray for the
    light,
And men in the suburbs who pray for the night;
And they're all trying to climb to the top of the
    mine,
And all of them say most of the way,
Screw you.

I worked in the mill from seven till nine,
Tears in my eyes nearly drove me half-blind,
Trying to make wages that weren't even there,
Taking hell from a foreman with the build of a
    bear.

He said, Screw you,
This is all you'll ever do,
It's the only existence for someone like you.

JACK-RABBIT

Go, jack-rabbit, running through the wood,
You had a good night and you feel real loose,
Heard they got you going round the goosecreek
    shed,
Trying to fill your belly full of buckshot lead.

Go, jack-rabbit, get the cabbage patch,
Farmer left the back porch door on the latch,
Heard you coming and he got his gun,
Better go, jack-rabbit, better start to run.

Go, jack-rabbit, running through the woods,
You had a good night and you feel real loose,
Gunfire breaking up the peaceful night,
Jack-rabbit lying in the cold daylight.

HO, HO, HO (WHO'D BE A TURKEY AT CHRISTMAS?)

Sitting here on Christmas Eve with a brandy in
    my hand,
Oh I've had a few too many and it's getting hard
    to stand,
I've been hearing noises from the fireplace,
I must be going crazy or the brandy's won the race.

And I keep hearing
Ho ho ho, guess who's here,
Your fat and jolly friend draws near,
Ho ho ho, surprise, surprise,
The bearded weirdy's just arrived.

On my roof there's snorting sounds and bells
    inside my head,
My vision's blurred with colour and all I see is red,
There's a pair of large-size wellies coming down
    my flue,
And the smell of burning rubber, oh, is filling up
    the room.

And I keep hearing
Ho ho ho, guess who's here,
Your fat and jolly friend draws near,
Ho ho ho, surprise, surprise,
The bearded weirdy's just arrived
(and here he is).

133

ROCK ME WHEN HE'S GONE

Warm the wine and give it to me
One more time again,
I'm just a rolling stone
Who needs a drop of rain;
And to taste your honey, Mona,
Is like lickin' on the sun,
My truck's hid in the back yard,
So come here and give me some.

Said lady, That's the way,
You've gotta to rock me when he's gone,
You make me feel like a diesel train going home,
We got so much to give each other
And we've only just begun.
So take me, baby,
Break me, lady,
Gotta rock me when he's gone.

Break the bread in two,
And you can give me half,
I've ridden hard and fast
Just to make you laugh,
To make you laugh
I've stood knee-deep in mud outside your door
Clutching in my hand a border rose from
    Baltimore.

THE LAST GOOD MAN IN MY LIFE

Think the trees are shedding leaves,
It looks that way and I might say
The same applies to me.
'Cause it's autumn in my heart,
And you're the reason, dear,
I should try to get you back
Instead of sitting being silly here.

'Cause you're the last good man in my life,
You left me half the woman that I was,
But I'm gonna find the time,
And you bet I'm gonna climb
Back into the arms of the last good man that I
    loved.

Could have been me acting smart,
But you know how I can't end
What I usually start;
You'll realize something's gone,
Sure hope you miss me then,
Oh, but I wouldn't make a fool of you,
I'd just pray that you might stay with me again.

136

LONNIE AND JOSIE

Me and Lonnie thumbed down a Cadillac
Outside Laredo in the heat of the sun,
The driver was tanned and he looked like a
    salesman,
We were just children on the run.

He talked real funny like we'd never heard,
Must have been foreign I guess,
And I felt like an actress in an old movie
As Lonnie and I drove west.

We were saying goodbye to the ones left behind,
Hello to the ones up ahead,
Lonnie and me were just drumming our knees,
While the radio D.J. said —

Keep your eyes open for Lonnie and Josie,
Sixteen and fourteen, playing hookey from
    school,
Last seen they were walking the road by the
    courtroom
Downtown Laredo at a quarter past two.

Our friend in the front seat turned around and
    smiled,
Grinning and shaking his head,
Asked us politely where we were going,
Where the sand turns to sea on the coast, I said.

We were crossing the border just out of Texas,
Passed the last dusty abandoned old farm,
With the A.M. playing the songs of Sinatra,
And Lonnie sleeping in my arms.

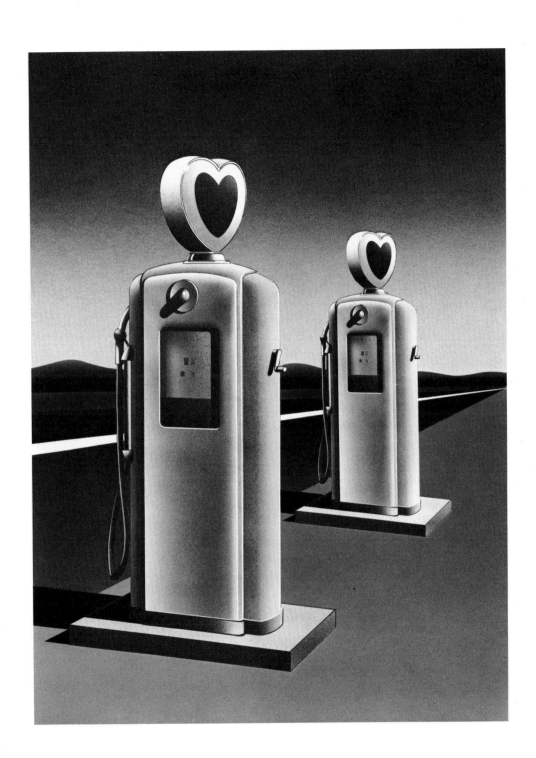

Bernie Taupin The One Who Writes The Words For Elton John

138

SING ME NO SAD SONGS

I know you, you're trying to do
All you can for me,
And I appreciate your help
But it's best just to leave me be.

There's many things that I have done
And I'm sorry for them now,
So darling, please don't you comfort me,
I'll sort it out somehow.

So sing me no sad songs
Tell me no lies
Please don't you make me blue.
Sing me no sad songs
Tell me no lies
Girl, I can do without you.

Don't go breaking my heart
It will tear me apart
Then I'll be finished for good.
Sing me no sad songs
Tell me no lies
Please don't you make me blue.

I don't want you to think I'm mean
Refusing all your help,
But the time has come
When my need is none
And I wanna be alone with myself.

SUPERCOOL

You came walking by where I was sitting pretty,
Said, 'Hey, babe, do you want to dance with me?'
And I noticed that you acted kind of funky,
As if somehow you were trying to be

Supercool, no one's fool, just a rolling stone
Acting out your party piece
In Valentino tones.

Smoking untipped cigarettes
And calling me a doll,
Sometimes I really wonder
If you're happening at all.

Oh, supercool, I gotta lose you
And your hip asides,
All this far out, right on, baby,
Teenage talking jive.

Supercool, go back to school,
Let's keep the whole thing clean,
As you would say in your sweet way,
You're really not my scene.

You cocked your brand-new felt hat to one side
Like Bogart used to do on the screen,
You've got to realize that I'm a big girl,
Older enough to know you're early in your teens.

139

CREDITS? WHAT DO
I WROTE THE WORDS.

EY MEAN, CREDITS?
AT'S IT, ISN'T IT?

CREDITS

ACKNOWLEDGEMENTS

With thanks to Royal Academicians Mary Barnes, Margaret Buck, Michael Craig, Ian Hay, Humphrey Ocean, Betty Swanwick and Jane Urquhart for permission to reproduce their work. Thanks to Bernie Taupin's mother for the loan of photographs of Bernie as a child, and a special thanks to Rosemary Corbridge who did an enormous amount of organizing and donkey work for this book.

BERNIE TAUPIN

was born on 22nd May 1950 on a farm near Sleaford,
Lincolnshire. The middle son of three brothers,
Bernie's father worked as a stockman for a local
landowner. When he was eight, the family moved to a
village with the unlikely name of Owmby by Spital and
Bernie attended Market Rasen Secondary Modern
School.

Despite showing flair for writing, when he left Bernie
worked for a printing firm, then as a farm labourer
running a chicken farm.

In 1967 he answered an advertisement in *New Musical
Express* for songwriters. Bernie's interest was purely
curiosity, but the result was one of the most famous
song-writing teams of this century. Elton John had
also written in. He could write music but not words;
conversely, lyrics came easily to Bernie, but not music.

Bernie now lives in Surrey and travels to the States a lot
with his American wife Maxine. His main interests are
books, films, and records, and this book came about
'To get everything I've done since I started writing
under one cover. It's just for my own satisfaction.'

P.S. . .

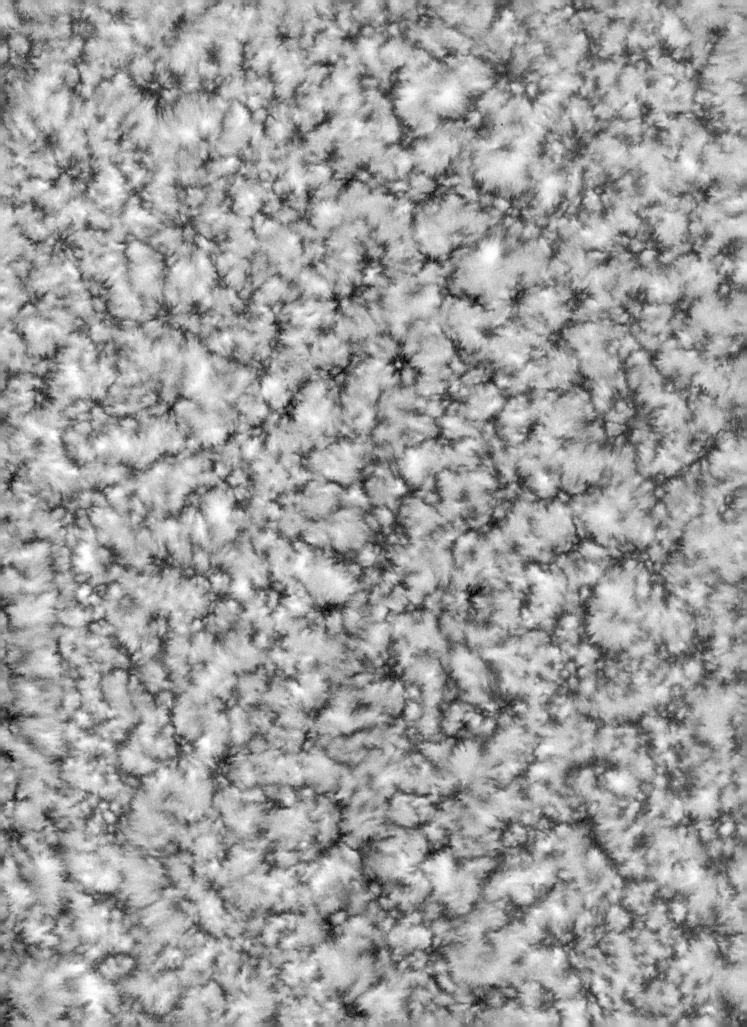

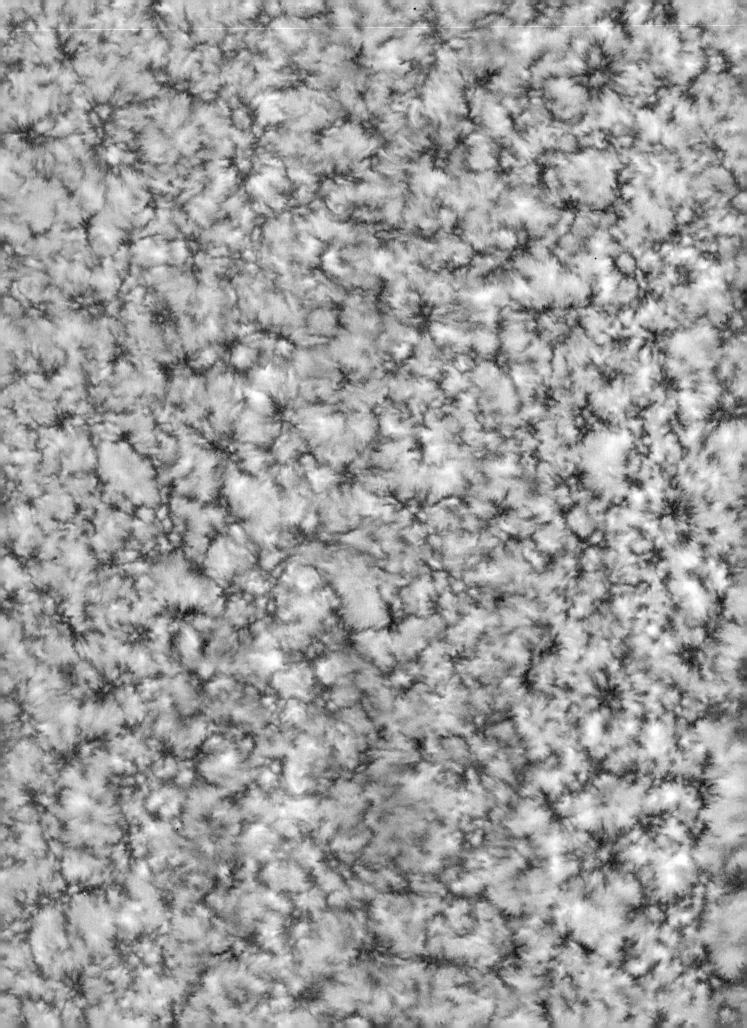